Kern River Country

Kern River Country

by Bob Powers

Illustrated by Jeanette Rogers

THE ARTHUR H. CLARK COMPANY
Spokane, Washington   1991

Dedicated to the best mother-in-law a fellow ever had, Ada Martin DaMant.

Acknowledgments

THE AUTHOR acknowledges, with deep thanks, the special aid and encouragement of: Dr. Rene Engel, Dr. Harland Boyd, Mary King, Bill Horst, Fay and Rulon Scott, Al Coe, Bob Reynolds, Alice Ingram, Marj Culley, Daisy Oldfield, Ben and Ruth (Fussell) Werth, Ken Wortley, Charles Henning, the Walker Rankin family and to Jeanette Rogers for the special work on maps and drawings. To my good friend Joan Dowd goes a great deal of credit for the many days she spent going over the manuscript.

Foreword

FOR CENTURIES the streams that coursed down the side of Greenhorn Mountain cut through the decaying rock, taking part of the mountain along as they tumbled their way down the Kern River.

Then in mid-18th century a Spanish doctor discovered gold among the sands of the river where it had been washed down from above. But it wasn't until the fall of 1854 that the outside world heard of the new El Dorado. Another gold rush was on!!

Although the excitement waned, and many miners left discouraged, some stayed on to raise families and crops along the Kern. Towns such as Keyesville sprang up, and, although it is only a monument now, for 100 years the area continued to attract those who could no more be kept from gold than a steer from a clover field.

A holdover from those rough and tumble mining days were the Shootin' Walkers. Their story rivals that of the feud between the Hatfields and the McCoys.

Dust from the freight wagons of the gold rush had barely settled when the Greenhorn trail was again brought alive by the dusty white tide of sheep. Their owners used this old emigrant trail as the first part of their yearly great circuit.

The Kern River Country story continues on down old Highway 178 with the mining town of Bodfish, and includes Miracle, Delonegha, and Democrat Hot Springs. The book closes with the building of Edison Company's Kern River Number 1 Power plant, and one of the most spectacular rescues of all time.

Table of Contents

I

Kern River El Dorado

THE DISCOVERY of gold at Sutter's Mill produced a new breed of men, whose lust for riches drove them to wander the mountains and deserts of the west, following their illusive dreams of wealth.

No matter where they hunted the yellow dust, they not only left their mark on the land but on the people they met, the towns they passed through or built, and on the economy and history of the entire country.

They were rarely discouraged enough to quit. Every claim that proved worthless only served to make them more determined to try the next gulch, the next mountain, or the next river. The stories of their strikes and their failures spread far and wide, and no matter how far-fetched the stories might be, they provided new hope to the gold-hungry miners whose "big strike" had eluded them.

It was one of these stories that brought Lewis Anderson, Theodore Stallo, David James, and Louis Robidoux to the Kern River country. The men left their homes in Millerton, California, in the spring of 1853. They traveled south to Visalia, through Linn's Valley and Poso Flat, then across Greenhorn Mountain and down the ragged gulches to the Kern River. They prospected along the Kern for several miles without success then moved east through the South Fork Valley and over Walker's Pass to the Mojave Desert in search of the Dead Mexican Mines.

One of the many widely spread stories that circulated among the miners in 1853 concerned a Spanish doctor who arrived in Mariposa with a sack of gold nuggets that he claimed to have found in a region "somewhere near the headwaters of the Kern." According to the doctor, he and four companions had found a claim that was literally paved with gold, the nearby hills turned yellow with rich outcroppings. While the miners were loading the gold nuggets into sacks and gloating over their new found wealth, a band of Poso Indians attacked them and killed all but the doctor, who escaped and made his way into Mariposa. The doctor attempted to organize a large enough party to return to the rich claim, exterminate the Indians, and bring out the gold.

The end of the story was vague but not enough to stop the Millerton miners from trying to to locate the Spanish doctor's discovery site. They searched for many months without finding a single trace of the claim. Finally they gave up, and returned to Millerton in 1854.

Other stories, equally improbable, spread throughout the state during the years after the gold rush of '49. There was some speculation that the rumors were purposely encouraged by merchants who were overstocked with mining supplies and by transportation companies whose businesses suffered when the first big rush of men and equipment slowed down.

The continued rumors of gold in the Kern River country brought another group of miners across the Greenhorn Mountains to the Kern River in the spring months of 1854. Headed by William Skinner, C. K. Worland and William Packard, the prospectors explored several areas on the river and decided to set up sluices and work a sand bar below Keyesville, which they called Elbow Bar.

They opened the claim after obtaining materials and supplies at great expense, including tackle and derricks to raise the large boulders that were imbedded in the bar. They labored long and hard throughout the summer to make their claim pay off. They finally abandoned the

Panning at Elbow Bar.

Heading for the Kern River El Dorado.

project because it was financially impossible to remove the gold from the large quantities of black sand because the gold was so fine.

Always hopeful, the prospectors moved down the river, joined forces with twenty or thirty other miners and together they worked along the bars and river banks, with varied success, into the winter of 1854.

On December 27th this group of miners, one of whom was William Skinner, discovered placer gold near the bottom of Greenhorn Gulch, and despite the December cold, about this same time another group of miners, including Theodore Maltby, Moses Kirkpatrick, George Baylor and Ezekiel Calhoun, crossed the Greenhorn Mountains headed for the Kern River. On about the same day that the miners at the bottom of Greenhorn Gulch discovered gold, Calhoun discovered placer diggings at the top of the Gulch, and that group staked claims on Bear Trap Flat. This was about three miles above where William Skinner made his discovery.

The news spread quickly among the men working along the river, and by January 10, 1855, all the miners working in that region had located a claim and were successfully mining gold.

THE GOLD RUSH WAS ON!

In the old pueblo of Los Angeles, 150 miles away, the news of the gold strike hit like a cyclone. The gold rush in the remote Kern River country would prove to be of great profit to the struggling Southern California town, still in the throes of a depression.

The sleepy cow country located in the gold rush area found itself suddenly transformed into bustling mining camps. An article dated February 8, 1855 announced, "Every description of vehicle and animal have been put into service by men in order to reach the goal of their hopes. Immense 10-ton mule wagons strung out one after another; long trains of pack mules, and men mounted and on foot with picks and shovels; boarding houses brought into requisition to take in the exultant seekers after wealth; keepers with their tents; merchants with their stock of miners' necessities and gamblers with their 'papers' are constantly leaving for the Kern River Mines.

"The wildest stories are afloat. We do not place reliance on these stories, however. If the miners turn out ten dollars a day to the man, everybody ought to be happy.

"The opening of these mines has been a god send to all of us as the business of the entire country had been on the point of talking to a tree."

Other exciting happenings, such as the discovery of a 42-ounce nugget in Rich Gulch (now Hungry Gluch and Boulder Gulch Campgrounds), gave the newsmen further reason to write jubilant reports. On March 7, 1855 the banner headlines read,

A gentleman miner heads for the Kern River mines.

In the four months following the announcement of the gold strike, over 5,000 men made their way into the Kern River Valley. The gold was there all right, but not nearly enough to go around. Though a few men struck it rich, many more struck nothing but hard luck.

By June, 1855 the retreat had begun. Most of the men who had ridden into the mines with high hopes, walked out on foot, discouraged. Only about 250 miners remained to work the placer claims.

In the rush of 1855, the largest number of miners arrived at the Kern River mines after the best claims had been staked. Claims varied in size. If the ground was very rich, each miner might only claim 100 square feet. If the ground was poor, the size of the claim was larger. A man's claim was held by leaving tools on the site and by working the claim continuously. A sign of honor in even the roughest of camps. If a dispute arose over the ownership of a claim, it was settled by a "jury" of other miners in the area.

If a miner was lucky enough to get one of the better claims on Greenhorn Gulch with water close by so that he didn't have to haul the gold-

A discouraged miner leaves the Kern River on worn shoe leather.

"Stop the press! Glorious news from the Kern River! Bring out the big guns! There are thousands of gulches rich with gold and room for 10,000 miners. Miners averaging $50 a day. One man with his own hands took out $160 in one day. Five men in 10 days took out $4500!"

A stream of miners was also pouring into the Kern River Mines through the San Joaquin Valley. The road was crowded from Stockton to the Kern River, a distance of 300 miles. Men traveled in stages, on foot, or horseback, on every kind of transportation that would help them reach the new El Dorado.

3

bearing dirt or sand to water, he could expect to wash about fifty pans of material in a ten-hour day and get between one-half ounce and one ounce of gold. At $16 an ounce, this gave him enough money to pay the inflated prices for food and supplies and to stash away a small amount for the trip back home.

Working on the Greenhorn slopes in early spring was a pretty chilly job for the men, particularly because they were damp most of the time from working in the mountain streams.

The days were hard, and the nights were not much better. Most of the miners carried a small roll of blankets to the gold fields, but even by sleeping with all their clothes on there were many cold nights spent shivering in their inadequate bedrolls, waiting for the sun to peep over the mountains so that they could begin another day of back-breaking labor.

In diaries handed down through the years, the men who challenged the Kern River country agreed that panning for gold was the hardest work they had ever done. They described the rigors of mining as being tougher than the combined ranch chores of ditching, canal digging, laying stone walls, ploughing, and hoeing potatoes.

The solid gold dream required a strong back and iron-clad determination.

The miners followed a regular routine. First, the gold bearing material had to be dug out, sorted, the most promising parts separated from the rest, and then washed. The key to all methods of separating gold in placer mining was the fact that gold was heavier.

Filling his pan with dirt, the miner held the pan partly under water and with a whirling wrist motion he washed loose most of the lighter material. Next, he raised the pan out of the water and continued the circular motion, punctuating the regular rotation with small jerks in and out of the water. This washed out the lighter sand and left only the gold. Many times the men would team up and one would dig out the gravel while the other did the tedious job of washing the gravel.

Although it was all called gold dust, it was found in many forms. Flour gold, which was as fine as yellow sand; coarse gold, which varied in shape and ranged in size from that of wheat kernels to the size of melon seeds; and lump gold, the nugget form which was the miner's dream.

Panning gold was not only the hardest method

A Kern River miner trying to make bacon and beans.

of mining, it also limited the amount of material that could be washed in a day because the pans were limited in size. The more material a miner could process in a day the more gold he could remove, so whenever possible the pan was abandoned in favor of the cradle or the long tom.

The cradle could be built in a few hours with about two dollars' worth of materials. But if the materials were as scarce as they were in the Kern River gold fields, a cradle could cost as much as one hundred dollars to build.

The cradle was simply an oblong wooden box about three feet long which was mounted on rockers. Bars, called riffles, were nailed along the bottom of the open end. An apron of canvas was stretched over a frame and placed inside the upper end of the cradle. A hopper with a piece of perforated metal in the bottom and a handle on the side was fitted over the canvas apron.

While rocking the cradle, the miner would pour water over the gravel in the hopper. After being strained through the hopper, the gravel was deflected by the apron, and as the water ran out the lower end of the rocker, the gold bearing sediment would be lodged behind each riffle and the lighter material was carried away with the water.

The miners soon discovered that the most efficient use of the cradle was obtained when four

Peter Gardett

men worked together. Two men would dig the gravel and carry it to the water, one would shovel it into the hopper and follow it with a bucket of water, and the fourth man would steadily rock the cradle back and forth. More material could be processed this way, more gold recovered and the proceeds were split four ways.

The long tom could handle even greater amounts of gravel. It was a twelve-foot-long trough, and water from a stream could be diverted through it. At one end of the trough was an uptilted, perforated iron sheet which was called a riddle. Loads of gravel were washed through the riddle, then dropped into a riffle box below where the heavier gold particles collected behind the bars.

The sluice box worked better than the long tom in places where there was a good supply of water. It was made by connecting a series of riffle boxes. Because of its length, the sluice box could process a lot more gold-bearing gravel than the long tom.

In 1855, the major mining settlement in the Kern River district was Petersburg. The miners in the area congregated there to pick up mail and supplies and to swap "gold" stories.

Petersburg was established by Peter Gardett, who was born in 1825 near Danzig, Prussia. Trained in navigation, Gardett followed the sea

for a livelihood. In 1851, his ship made its way around Cape Horn and berthed in San Francisco. Gardett had the heart of a true adventurer, and the exciting tales of the California gold rush lured him away from the sea into the gold fields of Mariposa County.

In April of 1855, Gardett joined the thousands of miners who swarmed into the Greenhorn district looking for a rich strike. He soon reasoned that there was more than one way to get his share of the gold, and that was by supplying food and equipment to the miners working nearby claims.

Gardett entered into partnership with Judge C. G. Sayles, and in short order he opened a store in a wooded section near Greenhorn Gulch, not far from the summit of the mountain. Supplies for the store had to be hauled into Petersburg over the rough Greenhorn Trail from Visalia, eighty miles distant.

The original site of Petersburg is shown on Forest Service maps to be about nine miles south of Greenhorn Summit, on Rancheria Road, just southeast of the Davis Guard Station Campgrounds.

Petersburg prospered as the Greenhorn Gulch miners continued to work their claims and the other miners, who were late-comers, spread out to locate gold deposits in other gulches and ridges in the vicinity. In 1858, a branch of the United States Post Office was established in Petersburg, with headquarters in Gardett's store.

The first postmaster was Alfred D. Hight, who had a ranch about one mile west of town, at the upper end of Freeman Gulch. In 1860, William Packard assumed the duties of postmaster. Packard, who was one of the original group of miners who discovered the first gold in 1855, was also a rancher with lands at the head of Greenhorn Gulch. The last postmaster in Petersburg was Harrison A. Rindge, who served from 1861-1863, when the post office was officially closed.

As mining operations spread out and moved further away from Petersburg, Gardett looked around for new adventure. He homesteaded land at Poso Flat, bought some stock, and built a log cabin. He divided his time and energy between his store and the land until 1860, when he sold the store and moved to Poso Flat to devote his full time to raising stock. His brand, the capital S, was the first brand to be recorded in Kern

County. In 1871, Gardett married Agnes Weber and took her to live in a new frame house at Poso Flat. There they raised two sons and two daughters.

Gardett sold the Petersburg store to Thomas Heston in 1860. Heston was new to the mercantile business, since he was known in the Kern River district for his efficient express service. The year 1860 was a busy year for Petersburg. To the great pleasure of the hard-working miners, Archibald M. Donaldson opened a bar and billiard saloon to take care of their recreational needs. Since Petersburg was a regular stop on the Greenhorn Trail, the saloon did a thriving business. A visiting editor of the *Visalia Delta* newspaper, James H. Lawrence, in commenting on the deplorable state of the roads into the Greenhorn mining district, mentioned Donaldson's saloon with wry humor, "People arriving here generally feel dry — no matter which way they come."

It is noteworty that Editor Lawrence, in an effort to get new subscribers and advertising from the mountain mining towns, changed the publication day of the *Visalia Delta* from Saturday to Thursday to accommodate residents in Keyesville, Petersburg, Linn's Valley, and intermediate points. According to Lawrence's notice to patrons on May 25, 1861, . . . "The stage leaves Visalia every Thursday morning and under our present arrangement our paper is nearly a week late by the time it arrives in Petersburg."

The change of publication date made it clear that the miners were quite important to the economy of the times.

Thomas Heston, who was a Pennsylvania Quaker, operated the store in Petersburg until 1862, at which time he sold it to Eugene Calliaud and turned all his interests towards building up his express business.

Heston came to the Kern River mining country in 1854 and started an express service between Keyesville and Stockton in 1855. In those early days, the U.S. mail, handled on contract by Heston, was carried from White River through Linn's Valley to Keyesville by mailriders. One of the first mailriders hired by Heston was Jim Dunlap, a teenager from Linn's Valley. In later years, he told many a tale about carrying the U.S. mail on a mule over the rugged mountain roads to Keyesville.

Heston owned lands in Visalia, and after he sold the Petersburg property in 1862, he opened a stage service between Visalia and Keyesville. He planned to extend the stage route into the Owen's River Valley to the Coso mining area as soon as the McFarlane Road (now Evans Road) was finished.

Well-known throughout the area, Heston entered politics and was elected to the State Assembly. Unfortunely, he became involved in "an affair of honor." According to a news story, he challenged a Visalia doctor to a gunfight. The doctor was killed, and Heston was wounded. In June of 1863, he left Visalia on a business trip to Fort Independence in the Coso region. On the return trip, he disappeared. Search parties were sent out to find him in July of 1863, but they were unsuccessful. Rumors of his murder were finally confirmed in August of 1864, a year later, when his remains were found about eight miles east of the J. V. Roberts ranch, in the Walker Pass area. Identification was made by papers found on the body, and by four teeth set in gold.

Thomas Heston died one year before the McFarlane Road was finished. His plans to enlarge his express route were left to others to complete, but he will always be remembered as one of the first pioneers to attempt to provide better means of transportation and better travel routes to the early residents of the Kern River and Greenhorn mining districts.

Transportation was a major problem for the pioneers who came in search of gold and stayed to settle in Kern River Country. An important part of the early legend is:

HOW THEY GOT HERE FROM THERE

It wasn't easy! In fact, the difficulties involved in traveling over the nearly impassable rugged mountains of the Sierra Nevada into the Kern River-Greenhorn mining area was the first test of endurance that faced the gold-hungry prospector.

Those men coming from San Francisco and other parts of the northwest traveled south through Stockton to the settlement of Visalia, which became the "jumping-off" place for miners and merchants heading for the Kern River gold fields.

From Visalia, a stage route carried passengers, mail, and supplies to Laver's Crossing in Linn's Valley, a distance of 68 miles. The road was

The Lavers hotel in Linn's Valley. Reverend O. D. Dooley, left, and David Lavers, right, pose in front of the hotel. From Laver's Crossing to the Kern River mines, the trail was rugged and it was every man for himself.

adequate, and stage travel was fairly comfortable.

However, from Laver's Crossing it was every man for himself, since the only way to reach the mines was either by mule or on foot over the rocky and treacherous Greenhorn Trail.

To aid unsuspecting travelers who planned to continue by stage to the mines, William Marsh and William Kennedy provided a string of riding and pack mules at Laver's Crossing, to travel back and forth across the Greenhorn Trail. Quite a few wagons braved the narrow, rutted trail from time to time, but despite its heavy use, the ravages of winter snow and spring rains kept it in constant disrepair. It never was considered much more than a ragged trail.

Originating at Laver's Crossing, the Greenhorn Trail wound south along Poso Creek to Poso Flat. Turning east up through Poso Flat it

scaled a ridge south of what is now called Eugene Grade, and crossed the summit about one-quarter mile south of where Eugene Grade now ties into Rancheria Road. From that point, the trail continued east to the settlement of Petersburg.

The last ten miles of the Greenhorn Trail, between Petersburg and Keyesville, was mean, steep and treacherous. Leaving Petersburg, the trail followed broken country east across the tops of Greenhorn Gulch and Bradshaw Gulch, and then dropped down into Black Gulch in a flurry of rocks and dust. Road builders and trail blazers of the day carved the way along ridges and razorbacks, cutting trees and stacking boulders as they went along, to make way for wagon wheels and heavily laden mules. One traveler commented, "The difficulties on this side (from Laver's Crossing to Petersburg) sink into insignificance when compared to the descent to Keyesville. To a person unaccustomed to mountain passes it looks like an incredible feat to take a wagon down this trail without smashing things."

Indeed, it was a feat! All heavily loaded wagons coming down this steep path "rough-locked" their wheels, using chains through the spokes so they wouldn't turn, and often tied a tree to the back of the wagon to slow it down. In addition, many teamsters carried a wagon shoe for each wheel. The shoes, shaped like a 12-inch iron sled, were fastened under the rough-locked wheel to reduce wear and tear on the wheels.

The trip uphill wasn't much better. William H. Brewer, a member of the famed Whitney Survey party, reported passing several Army wagons working their way up the trail from Black Gulch to the top of Greenhorn. His journal recorded that the Army was forced to double up their six-mule teams just to pull the empty wagons to the top.

In Black Gulch, the Greenhorn trail eased up a bit, passed by the site of what was later known as the Hawthorne Place, then crossed the Mammoth Ridge, and continued downhill to Keyesville.

Early in 1855, William Lynn started hauling hay from his Linn's Valley ranch, and other supplies, over the Greenhorn Trail to Keyesville. He didn't make many trips before he decided that he could build a better road by staying north of the existing trail. He also figured that he could offset the cost of the road by charging a toll to other teamsters who used it. Lynn's Bull Road also originated at Laver's Crossing, but followed Lumreau Creek a short way, then turned east, and after reaching the summit of the ridge just south of Rhymes Campground it followed the general route of Rancheria Road south to the present day site of Evans Flat Campground. From here it turned east to Keyesville. The descent to Keyesville was not much better than coming down the Greenhorn Trail. Lynn's Bull Road was finished in the latter part of 1856, and while it was better than the Greenhorn Trail, particularly for wagons, it still left a lot to be desired for travelers. Stretches of it are still visible in 1978, including sections which paralleled Lumreau Creek and presented grades of forty degrees or more.

These steep pitches on the road provided extra income for enterprising teamsters, who charged $25 to hook their yokes of oxen to heavily loaded wagons and help them to the top.

The "bullwhackers," as they were called, walked alongside their teams, armed with goads and bullwhips. A pop of the whip could be heard as far as a pistol shot. Some of the drivers who took wagons over the early roads were James Dunlap, William Josiah Ellis, and Gallant Brown. It was a local joke that when Gallant Brown came down off the Greenhorn, you knew he was coming! He could be heard for miles around, roaring at his bulls and cracking his whip as he plunged down the trail.

One of many stories about the "turrible road" came from Leila Stone, whose grandfather was William Josiah Ellis. He told her on one wild trip into Keyesville when the bulkhead on his wagon gave way and spilled the contents of his load down over the backs of his oxen. He lamented on behalf of all the teamsters who had to make the long trip to the Port of Stockton for supplies, because the trip always started and always ended with "that nightmare of a mountain."

In 1859, the *Visalia Delta* took a stand on behalf of the Greenhorn-Kern River travelers. After an eventful trip over the roads, the editor wrote, "This section of the country is sadly in need of better roads. There is a good wagon road to Linn's Valley, but from thence to the mines there is nothing but a mule trail over which everything has to be packed on the backs of animals. The citizens are now asking the county to assist them in building a road from Linn's Valley to the mines. They are willing to incur two-thirds of the expense of the road if the county will appropriate the other one-third. They have been paying taxes for years, and have as yet received no immediate benefit from those taxes. We hope that the Board of Supervisors, in their next session, will take this matter under consideration."

In 1861, John McFarlane, William Poer, and Peter Goodhue got into the road "show." They secured the services of Thomas Baker, considered to be the finest surveyor in Tulare County at the time. Baker, for whom the town of Bakersfield was later named, laid out such a good route that it is still being used 116 years later as the major access between Glennville and Wofford Heights. It is known as Evans Road.

Construction on the Mcfarlane Road began in

1861, at which time ninety percent of all traffic into the Kern River and Greenhorn area was forced to use either the Greenhorn Trail or Lynn's Bull Road. In 1862, Thomas Heston's Express Company began operating between Visalia and Keyesville, and also carried travelers into the Owens Valley east of Walker's Pass where new gold strikes were being made.

Amos O. Thom's Telegraph Stage Company operated between San Francisco and Visalia in 1862-63 and made connections with Heston's stage out of Visalia. The two companies provided a five-day trip between San Francisco and the Owens Valley Coso Gold Mines.

Parts of the McFarlane Road were ready for wagon traffic in 1863, and by 1864 it became a regular stage route which afforded good roads from Visalia to Whiskey Flat, Keyesville, and the Owens Valley.

Transportation continued to be a major concern as the Kern River Valley grew into a populated farming and mining community, but the pioneers of those early roads earned a salute for their perseverance.

BACK TO THE MINES

Mining in the Greenhorn district continued to flourish in 1856. The prospectors followed the natural flow of the mountain streams and mined the rich surface deposits that had been left there over the years. As the placer mining played out, the miners with more experience began searching for the original source of the gold.

When they located the first outcroppings of a gold-bearing quartz, they began digging shallow holes from which they removed the ore in buckets and broke it up by hand using a mortar and pestle. When the ore was ground finely enough it was mixed with water and the gold was separated by using a rocker.

As the miners burrowed deeper into the quartz veins, they had to handle tons of material instead of just bucketfuls, and they looked for other ways to work large amounts of ore more efficiently. Since the initial problem was finding a method of large scale crushing, the miners' solution was the use of the arrastra and the Chile mill.

The arrastra was Mexican in origin and had been used in grinding silver ores for hundreds of years. It was built by laying down an eight-foot circle of flat rocks surrounded by an 18-inch high stone wall. A post was set in the center, held

firmly by stonework. The center post supported a large pole or sweep, fitted with a chain or cable to which one or more heavy, abrasive rocks were attached. A blindfolded mule or horse was hitched to the end of the sweep and was driven around and around the outside of the arrastra while the ore on the inside was slowly pulverized.

Before being placed on the bottom of the arrastra, the ore was broken into chunks about the size of a man's fist. When the ore looked as though it was crushed finely enough, the miner would take a pinch of the material and rub it against his ear lobe. If it didn't scratch, it was ready.

The Chile mill was similar to the arrastra except that the ore was crushed beneath a large circular stone wheel which was about 7 feet high and about 1½ feet thick. The stone wheel was pulled around in a narrow trough by mule power in much the same manner as in the arrastra.

Once the ore was finely crushed, the next step was a process called amalgamation. It was not a new process to the miners of the 1850's since it had been used as far back as the 1500's as the simplest and cheapest method of extracting gold from crushed ore.

In amalgamation, the finely crushed ore was mixed with water and mercury, also called quicksilver, and stirred very thoroughly so as to break up the mercury into tiny particles which attracted all the fine gold. The pulpy mixture that resulted was then squeezed through a chamois bag to remove all the excess water and mercury. The remaining mass formed a heavy mercury-gold substance called an amalgam or alloy, which was often washed again to remove any trace of ore sands.

The mercury-gold amalgam was then placed in an iron vessel called a retort which was heated until the mercury was distilled into a vapor. The vapor rose into a tube or pipe, which was directed into a cooling chamber, where the mercury returned to its original state and was saved to use again. The gold was left in the retort. It was not pure gold at this point, but a rather spongy substance that contained some silver and other minerals. It was formed into balls or bars and sent to the mint where all the impurities were removed.

The number of quartz lodes being worked continued to rise, and with each new discovery

9

Crushing ore in an arrastra.

the miners faced the dilemma of working with increasingly greater amounts of ore. Eventually, the arrastra and the Chile mill were impractical for handling the many tons of raw material, and the miners turned to stamp mills.

The stamp mill originated in Europe and was introduced into the United States in the Southern Appalachian gold mines many years before the discovery of gold in California. Miners who had seen the stamp mill in operation in the east before they headed west to make their fortunes in the new El Dorado, designed the first crude stamp mills used in California.

The stamp mill, or battery, was built on the same principle as the mortar and pestle and was probably so named because the primary function of the stamp mill was to stamp or smash quantities of quartz ore into fine particles.

Many variations of the European stamp mill were built in the Kern River-Greenhorn mining districts in the year following the discovery of

gold. The earliest mills were constructed almost entirely of wood and varied in size from one stamp to twenty stamps. Four or five stamps was the average number used in local mills.

Whenever possible the mill was built on the side of a hill, near a stream, to allow the ore to move through the progessive milling steps by gravity fall and to take advantage of natural power sources.

In the ten-stamp mill illustrated, (see pages 12 and 13), a wooden frame held square wooden posts called stampers or stamps. Each stamp was fitted with a square iron shoe on the bottom and weighed about 250 pounds. The stamps were arranged in a row in a long, narrow trough called a mortar, into which ore and water were constantly fed by the millman. The stamps were raised by a camshaft and let fall in rotation, such as 1-3-5-4-2.

The action of the stamps reduced the ore and water into a pulp, which was forced through a

10

wire mesh screen with each surge of the powerful stamps. The pulp fell onto an incline table, built of rough planks, over which flowed a continual supply of water.

A series of wood strips, called riffle bars, were nailed across the table so that as the pulp was further reduced by water flow, the heavier gold particles lodged behind the riffle bars and the lighter ore sands were carried away. Just below the upper riffle bars was a set of smaller bars called Hungarian riffles. Mercury was placed behind the Hungarian riffles to catch the fine gold dust. At the bottom of the table, a strip of fabric such as velvet, corduroy or even a strip of blanket, was attached so that the rough nap of the fabric caught the finest flour gold which might have escaped the other sets of riffle bars.

Every four or five days the mill was shut down and the water flow halted for a "clean-up." Each riffle was carefully cleaned out and materials left behind the bars were panned to free the heavier gold particles. The Hungarian riffles were scooped free of their mercury-gold-sand mixture and the fabric at the bottom of the table was brushed clean and washed out and the fine gold sands mixed with mercury. The last steps of separating the mercury-gold amalgam were carried out by hand in the same manner as the miners used with the fine ore from the arrastra. It was definitely not a production line process.

In the wooden ten-stamp mill pictured, several sizes of ore could be handled at the same time, which increased production. A good millman could do some pre-sorting of ore as he fed it into the mortar. The first five stamps processed the finer gravels, and the second battery of five stamps crushed larger ore chunks.

The fact that this early mill had very little way to classify or sort sizes of sands was one of the main reasons that many failed to get all the gold from the ore. The material was not sufficiently broken down, and instead of being caught behind the riffles, the gold was washed off the table with the tailings.

About sixty percent of the gold in the ore was recovered by the amalgamation process, and the ten-stamp mill could crush about eight tons in a 24-hour period, depending on the size and nature of the ore. In 1856, the quartz ore was paying from $20 to $100 per ton, with an overall average of $60 per ton.

The power to operate the stamps and other mill parts was obtained in a number of ways. The most practical method was to use water from a nearby stream or river. With pipe, flume or an open ditch, the water was diverted from the stream to the mill and used to turn a water wheel which, in turn, generated power. Sometimes, the water was directed to turn a turbine, which produced power for the machinery. When the water supply was insufficient to turn either a water wheel or a turbine, there was usually enough to produce steam for boilers. Early stamp mills on the Greenhorn district were most often powered by steam, since the waterflow varied greatly, and there was a vast stand of timber to supply wood for the steam boilers.

The use of steam power created a great need for fuel. For miles around the mill, the countryside was stripped of all kinds of wood to feed the steam boilers.

Evidence of the indiscriminate use of all the timber in mill areas is quite obvious in 1979. The lands surrounding the Big Blue mill site, between Kernville and Wofford Heights, are almost completely devoid of trees. Also in Hot Springs Canyon and Cyrus Canyon, both of which lie east across the Kern River, one can still see the stumps of hundreds of juniper trees which were fed to the steam boilers, even though it has been 95 years since the steam hoisting works for the mine was destroyed.

Many miners found that there was too little profit in working a quartz vein alone, so they banded together to form companies. Other miners devoted their energies to building and operating the stamp mills and arrastras, both on Greenhorn and along the Kern River. By 1858, there were seven mills on the Kern River, two on Greenhorn Mountain, and a score of arrastras.

James W. Freeman and William C. Ferguson built one of the first mills on the Greenhorn, about two miles west of Petersburg on Freeman Gulch. In November of 1859, their mill was running one battery of four stamps. Plans were to attach another battery of four stamps, which would make the mill capable of crushing six tons of ore in a 24-hour period.

In 1856, quite a few Frenchmen appeared in the Greenhorn district to work a sizeable quartz claim staked by one of their countrymen, Dr. Claude de la Borde. Three of the French miners were Jean B. Courviere, Theophile Drago, and Jean Boissear. History records that the French

A Feeder Apron
B Water
C Wooden Stamps
D Mortar
E Screen
F Rotating Cam
G Table
H Upper Riffles
I Hungarian Riffles

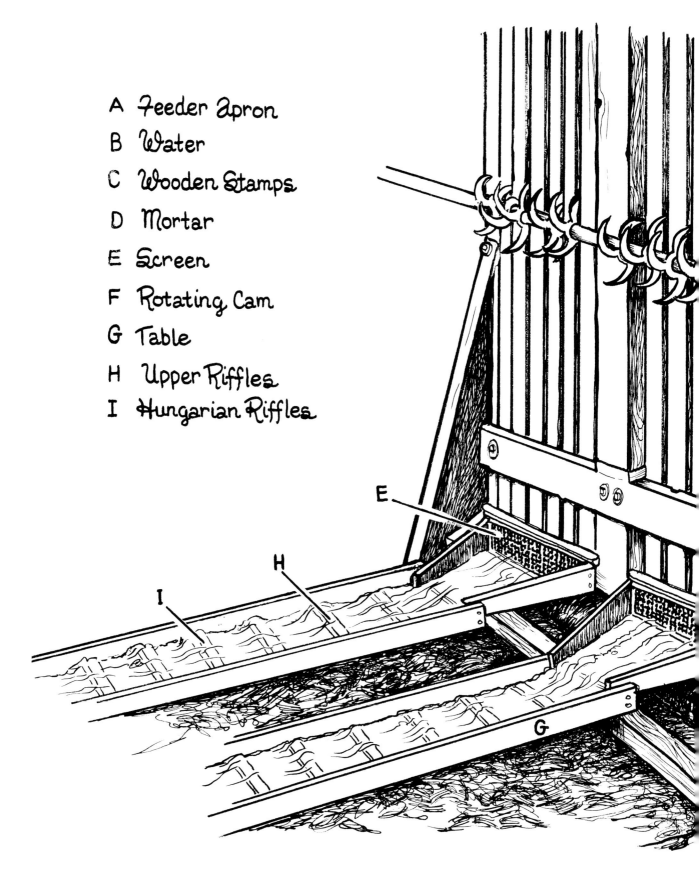

Early Stamp Mill

A miner operates a Chilean mill.

miners preferred the Chile mill to the arrastra and that they seemed to do better financially than their American counterparts. No doubt they worked harder and squandered less time and money in Mr. Donaldson's saloon in Petersburg.

One of the largest mining companies in the Greenhorn Mountain Mining district was the Alpine Gold and Silver Mining Company. By 1866, the company had acquired 53 quartz lodes and erected a twenty-stamp mill. On August 10, 1866, a mining periodical reported that the firm was employing 80 men and had 500 tons of ore ready for crushing.

Some of the successful mines in the area were the Rough and Ready, the United States, the Fairmont, and the Hope. Later strikes included the Lone Star and the Mayflower.

While Petersburg catered to the needs of the mountain-top miners in the Greenhorn mining district, another mining camp was established on the Kern River by the prospectors who made the

first discoveries at the bottom of Greenhorn Gulch.

Beginning with that first strike in January of 1855 until the early fall of 1855, mining operations continued to spread east in a ten-mile radius. Every gully and ridge eastward from Delonegha Hot Springs rang with the sound of pick and shovel. Placer mining produced many rich strikes along the Kern River, and miners dug deeply into the quartz ledges of the Kern River drainage.

Richard M. Keyes, a miner from the White River area, was among the first prospectors to discover a rich quartz vein, called the Keyes Mine, about ten miles from Petersburg in Hogeye Gulch, just above the Kern River. Soon after Keyes' strike, Capt. Theodore Maltby located another large quartz ore lode on the ridge between Hogeye Gulch and Black Gulch, which was named the Mammoth Mine.

The center of activity in the area known collec-

14

Spanish arrastra — Keyesville.

tively as the Keyesville mining district, became the camp town called Hogeye or Keyesville.

Remains of a Chilean mill used in 1856 in the Keyesville Mining District was located near one of the dry gulches above the river.

KEYESVILLE

By 1856, Keyesville had been laid out in a rather haphazard manner, but with all the signs of fledgling township. Surrounded by the grey granite cliffs of the Sierra Nevadas, a shabby collection of a dozen or so tents and shacks with dirt floors provided the bare necessities of community living to the miners working nearby. The men were too consumed with gold fever to be much interested in their living conditions. However, once a camp town was established, merchants appeared like magic to set up shop and relieve the miner of some discomforts and a good bit of gold dust.

The first storekeepers in Keyesville were the industrious twosome, William Marsh and William Kennedy. They were soon joined by John Kelso, Thomas Rothschild, and Adam Hamilton. The latter gentleman soon left the dingy mining town to set up a bar in Whiskey Flats, forerunner of the town of Old Kernville.

James Scobie and William Scodie established eating houses in early Keyesville to supplement

William Scodie

the miners' diet of hardtack and beans. Scodie continued to serve the public after he left Keyesville by opening a way station in the South Fork in 1861. The station still stands in 1979 as a familiar landmark, the Onyx Store.

Salt pork was the main meat in the miners' diet, since they rarely took time off from their claims to hunt wild game. But there were several hunters who managed to make a few dollars by bringing fresh meat into the Keyesville mining camp. Probably the most colorful hunter to pass through the gold country in 1855-56 was James Capen Adams. Adams has been immortalized by the television series, "Grizzly Adams." Adams hunted deer and bear in the nearby mountains and sold the meat to miners in the area. With Adams when he came into the Kern River country were his two pet grizzly bears, Lady

Washington and Ben Franklin. Lady Washington was kept chained to his wagon, but Ben ran loose with Adams' dog, Rambler.

The miners who didn't want to bother with building a shack found lodgings with George McKay, Benjamin Miller, or Myron Harmon. "My," as he was nicknamed, also ran a blacksmith shop and cut lumber with a whipsaw to build the first houses in Keyesville. He split shakes that were used for roofing and sometimes for the walls of some of the early dwellings.

Those first days of Keyesville were marked with struggle, hard work, and a fair share of violence. There was little time for relaxation in the rough and rugged town, and drinking and gambling offered the only outlet for many men. The miner's law was his conscience, and tempers wore thin on more than one occasion. One of the first deaths to be recorded was that of Harris Casper in 1855. Casper was killed by an irate miner because he refused to sell the miner a pair of pants on credit. In 1856, Hopkins Stewart got into an argument over a card game. He fired the first shot, but missed, and was killed by the man he challenged. Stewart had been involved in several similar gunfights in Los Angeles, and his killer was not prosecuted on the grounds that he had acted in self-defense.

Excitement of a different kind livened things up in the early spring of 1856. William Lynn, who was finishing the last leg of the Lynn's Bull Road between the Greenhorn Trail and Keyesville, came high-tailing into town with the news that the Tule River Indians were on the warpath. Lynn was a man of action and he liked to be in the thick of things, so he rallied some of the miners and merchants together to form a posse to ride to the rescue of white settlers on the Tule River. Riding with Lynn were members of his road crew, and some of his neighbors from Linn's Valley, including Dave Lavers from Laver's Crossing. The posse numbered about sixty men.

As soon as the posse rode out to Keyesville, Theodore Maltby, who was the sub-Indian agent in the Kern River area, sent a rider to request military aid from Fort Tejon in the event that local Indian tribes decided to attack Keyesville. Alarmed residents also dispatched David Smith, the mail rider, with a letter to the sheriff in Los Angeles asking for help.

While they waited for aid, Frank Warren and

W. R. Bower, who later became a Kern County sheriff, organized a work force and began building an earthwork fort to protect Keyesville. The fort was nothing more than a hollowed out place on a knoll east of town. Shoulder high walls of brush were stacked along the perimeter and packed in place using the dirt removed from the hollow. It was large enough to protect 200 people, and the remains are still visible in 1978, just east of the historical marker at Keyesville.

As Keyesville prepared for attack, Lynn's posse arrived on the Tule River. There are as many stories about the events of the next few days as there were men in the posse, but the following account by Dave Lavers was recorded by Guy Hughes, a pioneer rancher.

According to Lavers, as the posse approached, the Indians — men, women and children — took cover on a nearby hill. They hardly looked like a band of Indian bucks on the warpath. Confused, Lynn decided that some action was better than none, so he ordered his men to make armor, using the heavy tarps that covered the loads on their pack horses. With the Indians surrounded, they spent most of the second day making armor. Lavers thought that Lynn was stalling for time because he wasn't anxious to attack a band of Indians that included squaws and papooses.

Lavers believed the whole uproar began when the Indians held a pow-wow to conduct tribal business, and the noisy gathering upset some nervous white settlers so much that they howled, "Attack."

On the third day, a non-commissioned officer and a private arrived from Fort Tejon to investigate the uprising. The officer looked over Lynn's armor and heard his plans for attack, but asked Lynn to hold off until he and the private could reconnoiter. Several hours later, the officer and his one-man army returned and announced, "You can go home, boys, the war is over — the Indians surrendered."

I imagine Billy Lynn's face was pretty red, but before he got back to his road camp another mis-adventure left it even redder.

While the posse broke camp, Lynn and Lavers headed back to Keyesville to tell the miners that the danger was over. Since they were both young and well-mounted, they rode hard and fast, and by dark they were also close enough to Lynn's Cold Springs road camp that they decided to ride on in. About a mile or so from camp, an indistinct

Myron E. Harmon

object confronted the two men in the darkness. Lynn shouted, "It's a bear, Dave, a bear — and we need meat!" Lynn aimed into the darkness, pulled the trigger, and the object fell, thrashed around for a second or two, then was still.

No one will ever know if they really needed meat in camp or whether Lynn just hated to make that long trip without even firing his gun once. However, the next morning when they returned in daylight to collect the "bear meat," they found the carcass of one of Lynn's work mules that had strayed away from camp. For Billy Lynn, it was one of those weeks that just started off bad, and continued downhill!

Keyesville improved its shabby looks throughout 1856, thanks partly to My Harmon's whipsaw. There were no formal streets, but cabins were perched in a semi-circle on one hillside and several rough-sided wooden stores housed the businesses down below. Mining was prospering, and the town grew.

A United States Post Office was established in 1857 with James Blackburn as the first postmaster, followed by Joseph Caldwell in 1858, William Kennedy in 1860, and Myron Harmon in 1862.

The town of Keyesville underwent a bit of "gentling," with the arrival of several families. This changed the atmosphere of the rowdy mining camp for the better. According to one reporter, ". . . as the women and children arrived, the loafers left and the rum shops went out of business." Naturally, a saloon or two survived, but there were definitely some changes.

Captain Abia Taylor Lightner brought his wife, Jemima, and their seven children to live in a new house on the hillside. He had come to the Kern River shortly after the first gold discovery. In 1856, he built the first stamp mill in Keyesville, worked several of the mines, and finally took over the Old Mammoth Mine which showed great promise.

Lightner had earned the title of Captain when he led a wagon train of settlers from Lancaster County, Pennsylvania, west to California in 1849. The trip took ten months, and the youngest of the Lightner children, Abia Jr., was born on January 1, 1850, when the wagon train reached Pomona, California. Lightner first settled in San Jose, then moved to a farm near Alviso which was quite successful. When it was time for the older boys to attend college, the Lightners moved to Santa Clara, where the boys entered the "Little Red Brick College" and Abia and Jemima took possession of a Baptist seminary and started a school. Lack of Baptist support doomed the venture, and the seminary became a boarding house for students attending the Catholic Mission College and the San Jose Convent. News of the Kern River excitement brought Abia to Keyesville, and after he bought the Mammoth Mine, he brought his family to live in the mining town.

Lavenia Lightner was nine years old when the family moved from Santa Clara to Keyesville in 1857. Her account of life in the mining town, written in 1936, reveals another side of the story.

"Being a child of but nine years when we came to Kern River, I can have little to tell, other than that which would interest children. All was very unlike the quiet little school, college and churchgoing village of Santa Clara. There were no racketeers and the noisy, exciting events were the wild pranks of the boys who attended the little red brick college.

"On our arrival at Kern River, we camped in a little log hut near a ferry run by Mr. Joseph Caldwell, until a house was prepared in Keyesville. Mr. Caldwell was a very sad looking, old man. He had a one room house and two children, a girl eight years old and a younger boy. There were few comforts in their home. The little girl tried to keep house, even to doing some of the cooking. We were very sorry for them.

"The river, dashing over rocks and eddying into whirlpools, with trout glistening in the water, was an endless amusement for us children.

"We soon moved into a new clapboard house in Keyesville. Here my father, who was following mining, had gold scales. Many miners would come with their gold dust, to have it weighed. They were generally rough looking men, with knives and pistols belted around them.

"We stood in awe of these men and would view them from our sheltered places. Their language, too, was rough. Father asked them in a kindly way, not to swear in his house. Always afterward they were very careful not to do so. They were not always careful in handling their gold dust and often scattered particles on the floor. Brother, Sis, and I would come from hiding when the men were gone and gather the gold dust left on the floor. We would often get a half a teaspoonful.

"There were wild times in the mining camps in those days, where men would be crazed from too much 'fighting whiskey' and mothers would gather their children into their own homes for safety.

"Keyesville had their bad men, too. Frank Warren and Claude Sales, when they were on their 'sprees'! They would, when drunk, stand out in the open, whirl their pistols around their heads and shoot, not caring in what direction.

"My brother-in-law, Frank Barrows, had an arrastra by the side of his dwelling and just when he bent over to attend the arrastra, a bullet passed over him and went through his house. My sister, who was outside, was too frightened to go in, fearing that the bullet might have killed her sleeping child, but the baby was not hit. Frank was a most peaceful man but this act angered him and he went to the saloon and told the men there that if the drunk men had any friends there, they had better take care of them, or he would. All the men were afraid of the two men, but some

Lavenia (Lightner) Rankin.

of the saloon people went out and got their guns from them and shut them up somewhere and all was quiet.

"We very much admired the beautiful crystallized quartz from the Keyes Mine, just filled with chunks of gold in the most fanciful shapes. I think no other mine in Kern County has ever produced such beautiful specimens.

"There were no schools or churches in Keyesville. Mrs. Keyes and my mother found a book of sermons and engaged a young Mr. Carrol, who was a very fine reader, to read a sermon each Sunday. Mary Keyes, the daughter, had a most magnificent voice for singing and led the hymns and all enjoyed it very much.

"There were very few children in Keyesville and not much amusement, but we loved to ride Old Bill, and a little sorrel pony we brought

across the plains, and Little Jim, a very gentle mule. One day Sis and I rode about a mile north of Keyesville to visit an old lady, Mrs. Blackburn. She was glad to see us as we were well fed and full of pep, but she thought we must be very tired and hungry after a mile's ride. She beat up some most delicious batter cakes and cooked them for us. Oh! they were so good. I seem to be able to taste them yet.

"Another thing which interested us very much were the bunches of Indians who came into town with their pickaninnies and dogs to beg or buy at the store. They soon found our house a good place to come to. They were always satisfied by food and other gifts. The chieftan, Jose Chico, and his family often visited us and named their two young daughters after my sister and me.

"A great event at that time was the arrival of the pack train with goods for Marsh and Kennedy's store. Old and young were interested. Children were sure of sticks of striped candy and fresh grapes packed in boxes of sawdust. They would come through in good shape. All supplies were brought in on pack mules at that time."

Lavenia Lightner lived to be 100 years of age; 90 of those years she spent in Walker's Basin. She married Walker Rankin Sr. and they pioneered one of the best farming and cattle ranches in Kern County.

The year 1857 was a good year in Keyesville. Miners were optimistic about the quantity of gold in the rich quartz lodes located all through the district; new mills were being built and new milling processes put into operation.

Richard Keyes had given up using an arrastra and had built a practical wood stem, hog trough, iron mortar stamp mill. He was seen coming into town after a day at his mill, carrying a small, battered bucket half-full of balls of gold bullion. Mining and milling costs were about $15 a ton, and the going price on quartz ore from Keyes Mine was $100 per ton. A very handsome profit.

Lightner was milling ore from the Mammoth and also doing custom mill work for other miners. He was quite excited about the show of gold in the Mammoth, and assured his family that his fortune was made. Prosperity seemed to be in the cards for all the Keyesville prospectors.

In a gesture of good will, the mining community allowed a small group of previously banned Chinese to work in the Kern River Mines under contract to the Americans. They were diligent

Some old time miners ham it up for the benefit of the cameraman.

workers, and lived off to themselves in a little settlement along Hogeye Creek. Many remained through the winter and into the next year to work claims of their own.

The business community, too, was thriving. Merchants were doing a brisk business with new families whose female members required a more varied selection of clothing, yard goods, and foodstuffs.

Another sign of growth was the new office of James W. Freeman, attorney at law. Freeman's office was located in the "business district" and made legal help available to all the residents. His official title included Justice of the Peace, but he could be called upon to settle land disputes or milling contracts. He became a state senator and, while a resident of Keyesville, he introduced the bill which led to the creation of Kern County. Still later, he was named as Kern County District Attorney.

Freeman slept in his office, called the "courthouse," and took his meals with the Lightner family on the hillside. It was one of the early morning duties of older Lightner boys to

step outside in the yard and heave a small rock onto the roof of the "courthouse" to summon Freeman to breakfast.

During 1857-58, other mills on the Kern River were built by Nathan L. Barrows and George H. Bodfish. The chief gold-producing mines in the Keyesville district were the Mammoth, Keyes, Scorpion, Lavenia and the Buckeye.

Toward the fall of 1858, gold production at the Mammoth dropped sharply; in fact, it failed entirely. Later owners would rediscover the rich leads, but for Abia T. Lightner the great dream of El Dorado came to an abrupt halt. He did not give up his dream easily, for even though he moved to Walker's Basin and began farming and raising stock, he kept returning to the quartz mines in search of "just one good vein of gold" until the fateful winter of 1861-62 when his mill was destroyed.

In 1859, a drought came to plague the miners, drying up streams and severely curtailing the water supply to power the stamp mills. The Kern River was the lowest it had been in four years, since the gold strike in '55. Many of the quartz veins that had been paying well had to be abandoned for want of capital. Those that were being worked were doing so on a limited scale because of the expense involved in getting the ore out. The successful veins that had been worked to a great depth required double the time and effort to get even half as much ore out as before.

There were about fifteen Americans on the Kern River that summer, and about the same number of Chinese. They were determined to survive. They opened up old placer sites along the river and worked the gulches and draws; they defied the drought and continued to labor in search of gold.

Keyesville was almost deserted in August of 1859. A visitor from Walker's Basin wrote this haunting description of the once lively, hopeful little town:

"'Tis a round hole shut out from the world, surrounded by hills. A few dingy, smutty homes which look up in mockery to the surrounding quartz lodes, as if to say, how long before you will belch forth enough of the wherewithal to erect houses in our stead. Every breeze heavily laden with the sweet scent of sagebrush blossoms, steals through halls of Indian Ranchera and finally wafts its obnoxious effluvia through the principal streets of this burg.

Robinson Brothers crushing quartz ore in a water-powered arrastra on a site near Tilly Creek in the early 1900's.

"And naught is heard save the humorous discord of green-headed bull frogs or the musical voice of the lonely Kiote, which keep up an incessant strain of their vocal powers the night through.

"The burg boasts of a Mercantile House, a Blacksmith Shop and a Dead-Fall. The latter being the general place of resort on the Sabbath where all congregate. While some are gassing about how rich they have struck it, others in a distant corner are giving and receiving instructions in Hoyle's surgery—and some gazing on in plentiful silence, wondering how 4 Aces are beaten with 3 Jacks and a doleful sound."

No matter how true, it was a sad picture of the Keyesville that had once seemed prosperous and hopeful.

Among the hard-headed prospectors, there was one man who found these grim days offered the opportunity to philosophize. His words were carried in the *Visalia Delta* on September 24, 1859. He wrote under a pen name, Idler.

"Time, the true developer of men and things is manifesting to the public mind of this place and vicinity, the truth, importance and wisdom of the aphorism, 'Make hay while the sun shines.' Had many followed this, they would not be where they are now. The most sagacious and far-sighted have had their minds bewildered and their judgements confounded and baffled at every turn in endeavoring to gain a respectable share of the 'filthy lucre' — more particulary so in mining, I think, than in any other pursuit. I speak from experience and observation.

"It cannot be denied that with all its elating influence and alluring prospects, the idea of suddenly being in possession of a fortune lacks that certain tangibility that ordinarily attaches to most other pursuits. It has great influence and weight upon the feelings and passions of men . . . for they will mine and continue to mine, so long as the universe holds.

21

"The fact is apparent, and stands indisputable, that at the present time everything here is in a most wretchedly collapsed state, and so profoundly so that it will require the most untiring perseverance and indefatigable energy, to ever give us a respectable position as a place. However, we still have hope and energy, and with these we may yet find ourselves at some future time prosperous and flourishing."

The drought continued, but so did the tenacity of a handful of miners . . . who still had hope and energy, and more importantly, a dream.

The editor of the *Visalia Delta* traveled to the Kern River in the fall of 1859 to reassure his readers about the activity in the gold mines. He reported as follows on November 24, 1859:

"From Petersburg it is ten miles to Keyesville, a rough road and mostly downhill. Keyesville is situated near the Kern River and about four miles below the forks. This was once a flourishing town but at present there are a few inhabitants, the miner being temporarily absent on the river during the summer. This is the last settlement and the most important place in the Kern River mines. There is gold in all the gulches around here, but there never has been water sufficient to work successfully after the first discovery.

"The mining here is especially in quartz, the leads being numerous all through the hills, some of which have paid as high as $600 to the ton in the old fashioned arrastras. There has been a large amount of gold taken out of the quartz here. Lately, they have erected mills running by water power, in which the quartz ore is crushed, but either the leads have decreased in value or their mills do not save the gold — in consequence of which many miners have become somewhat discouraged and left their quartz leads temporarily for the river mines.

"Mills in the vicinity are: First, Mr. Erskine and Sons on the opposite side of the river running two stampers. This mill is run by water power supplied by a spring. These gentlemen have expended much time and money in adding complicated machinery to their mill, all of which has proved a failure and they have returned to the original stampers with galvanized plates below the battery.

"The next mill is owned by Messrs Marsh and Co. running four stampers. Immediately above is the mill of Messrs A. T. Lightner and Co., four stampers, and nearby is that of Messrs Keyes,

also running a four stamper.

"All the mills have nothing but galvanized plates for saving the gold with the exception of the Keyes mill which has an ingenious contrivance in imitation of the Chilian Bowl which appears to work well. All the above named mills are run by water power supplied by the Kern River. About two miles above Keyesville are the arrastras of Joseph Caldwell (a spot known as Solitare) also run by water power. This gentleman deserves much credit for his ingenuity in devising and constructing the machinery he has in operation, which consists of five arrastras run by one water wheel. This is a new enterprise and the gentleman was testing the quartz from different leads to learn whether the fault was in the mills or the quartz. (We expect to be advised of the results of the experiment.) Should his experiment succeed it will give new impetus to mining around Keyesville.

"The location Mr. Caldwell has chosen for his mill site is one of the best on the whole river, possessing the advantages of a fine mill seat in a rich alluvial bottom capable of producing all kinds of grain and vegetables that can be produced in the state. In addition to this, there are large valleys on both branches of Kern River susceptible to cultivation and well adapted to grazing."

Joseph Caldwell had been most far-sighted when he located the tiny settlement of Solitare at the conjunction of the north and south forks of the Kern River. It had become the principal river crossing for all traffic since the first gold discoveries in 1855.

In 1856, Caldwell put in a ferry service at Solitare and charged a healthy toll to bullwhackers such as John Kelso, who crossed the river at Solitare to begin the 150-mile trek to Los Angeles. The route followed the South Fork of the Kern, through Kelso Canyon and Jawbone Canyon to the desert, then south across the desert through Willow Springs, Elizabeth Lake and into Los Angeles.

The only residents of Solitare were Caldwell and his two children; George Clancy and John Nicoll. Nicoll also had a blacksmith shop next to his home to service animals and wagons when they entered or left the Kern River mining district.

The largest meeting of miners ever held in the state of California took place in 1859 at the annual meeting of the Quartz Miners Association in Grass Valley (northern California). A long and heated discussion of mining problems brought no immediate answers to the dilemma of Keyesville prospectors. There was much talk of the "new" El Dorado in the Owens Valley beyond Walker Pass. There were many who warned that it was a hoax and others who were anxious to try a new field.

Charles Mixon, Boyd Braxton and Peter Swift joined the trans-Sierran excitement in 1859 and headed for the Coso Mines in the Mono Lake region to confirm the rumors of gold.

They returned to Keyesville late in the year with samples of the gold dust they had found. The three men had staked a claim on "Mary's Gulch" and worked it for 28 days. Using a rocker, cut with an axe out of a pine log, they washed out $2800 worth of gold dust between them.

It didn't take many of these tales to start the big rush into the Owens Valley, via the Caldwell crossing at Solitare.

Charles Worland, who had a ranch near Caldwell's millsite, recognized the opportunity at hand, and built a toll bridge at Solitare in 1859. On one particularly busy day, a group of 200 teamsters with 60 wagons carrying provisions and mining machinery, accompanied by some several thousand head of stock, jammed the crossing at Solitare.

The only other major river crossing was a toll bridge four miles downstream from Solitare. Benjamin Kelsey built the bridge in 1856 at a point just below where Erskine Creek now empties into the Kern River. It serviced the traffic heading south through Walker's Basin, passing by Caliente Creek and across the Tehachapi Valley to converge with the Kelso Valley trail north of Willow Springs.

Benjamin Kelsey was one of the first company of settlers to come across the plains from Kentucky to California in 1841. He was an adventurer and not satisfied to stay too long in one place. He sold the bridge to Michael Erskine soon after it was built, and Erskine operated it for the next few years. James W. Freeman, a Keyesville attorney, bought it at a sheriff's sale in 1860.

The dry spell continued through 1860 and then in 1861, early rains and a liberal spring runoff replenished the streams and the Kern River. Keyesville mining had reached a low ebb, but the few prospectors who had hung on

through the bleak, dry years were not discouraged, despite Nature's next ironical twist. Too much water. The town of Keyesville had evidently seen its heyday; it was once again populated mostly by miners and rough and tumble drifters.

In May of 1861, the following report of the Keyesville mining district appeared in the *Visalia Delta*:

"Keyesville, like other towns we read of, looks bigger on paper than it appears on its perch among the barren, granite-fastened hills by which it is environed. A view of its surroundings calls up reminiscences of the days of the great Kern River excitement, and visions of sore-backed mules and sore-footed miners, 'hurrying in hot haste,' flit before the imagination — and with them comes up the query of, what pitch of desperation must have seized upon the poor devil who first penetrated that forbidding spot in search of gold. Sand — granite boulders — here and there patches of cactus and dwarfish shrubs — more sand — and a great many more boulders, form the principal features of the mountain landscape.

"Those who had the energy and perseverance to dig for gold here should be entitled to no little credit. They have dug, however, and in many cases been rewarded, and even at this late day many are profitably working in quartz and placer diggings, although operations have been temporarily suspended in quartz, owing to the high stage of water on the river — the mills being situated on the bank — so near the stream that they are inconvenienced by back water. Several hundred tons of ore are ready for crushing and promise to pay well.

"Caldwell's Arrastra Mill is at present the only one in operation and he is grinding ore for the other parties at $8 per ton.

"Keyesville is destined, we think, to become a place of more importance than at present. The mineral resources around it will justify a population more than tenfold of that now employed in the vicinity, while its location — on the route of those who will return disappointed from the Coso Mines, is favorable for its future prosperity. At present there are 3 stores, 2 boarding houses and a blacksmith shop."

Hope for the bright return of Keyesville was evidently not just a miner's dream

After the setbacks caused by the dry spell, the

miners put on their thinking caps and came up with an idea to bolster the placer mining in the gulches, which always before was conducted only during the short rainy season. The plan was to build two water ditches. One was constructed by Summer and Co., the other by the Keyesville Ditch Co. Eight men financed the Keyesville Ditch operation which proposed to take water from tributaries of the North Fork of the Kern River and eventually from the river itself. The ditch was to be 20 miles long, with at least three miles of flumes, and would carry 1,200 inches of water to placer sites. Summer's ditch was reportedly finished before the fateful winter of '61 and '62, but the Keyesville Ditch Company's project faded into an uncertain future.

In the winter of 1861-62 all of California was drenched by heavy rains. Nature dealt another blow to the Kern River mining country, which suffered heavily from the prolonged storms. Keyesville was cut off from the outside world for a month, and it was late February before they could find out what had happened to friends in other parts of the county and report on the havoc that the floods caused in their own area. As always, their link with the *Visalia Delta* provided the sole means of communication. The following description of the flood appeared in the issue of February 20, 1862:

"This community (Keyesville) was thrown into ecstasies this evening by the arrival of the Visalia mail, it is the first mail; or in fact, the first communications of any kind that we have had with the outside world for four weeks. And in these times of flood, we have lived in perpetual anxiety for the fate of our friends in the Valley.

"The result of the flood is not as bad as we had anticipated however, for through indirect channels we have received accounts of the most serious disaster — loss of life, destruction of property and such.

"We have experienced something in the way of high water up this way. The river raised to the height of 50 feet above the low water mark. Impassable streams of water came gushing down from every canyon or gulch and with an occasional slide from the mountain, by way of giving effect to the picture.

"The loss of property on the river has been considerable. Both bridges that spanned the river at this place were swept away. All the quartz mills on the river were either swept away or materially damaged. First went the mill of Marsh and Co., then that of A. T. Lightner. Dr. de la Borde secured his mill for a longer time by the aid of braces etc. etc. But 'no go' or rather 'all go'. About this time certain cog wheels floating down the river gave notice that our enterprising friend, Caldwell, was also a contributor to the general confiscation of water lots. Of course, the batteries and heavy irons belonging to the first mentioned mill will be recovered. They will probably be rebuilt and possibly on a more improved style. The mill of M. Erskine and Co. was entirely swept away, not a vestige of it remained. Redfield and Son were more fortunate, for they erected their mill on a large sand bar. The institution is still there, but rather deep down, for an immense sand bar has formed over the site, covering it completely. This is reversing an ancient order regarding building on a sandy foundation with satisfactory results. Our old friend, Phil Wagy, has suffered by the freshet more severely than any other of the mountain farmers. His ranch being partly washed off by the torrents of water, and the remaining part being covered with a deposit not profitable for agricultural purposes. The cause of this disaster is owing to a slide from the mountain filling up the bed of the stream, the water forming in an immense reservoir above and after forcing its way through the obstruction, forbid all opposition.

"It was only by the most extraordinary exertions that Mr. Wagy succeeded in saving his family from the torrents of water. The crumbling of the mountain was described by those who say it was a really grand and terrific sight. Huge masses of mother earth gathering force as it went, came down the steep mountain declivity with wild and terrible confusion indescribable.

"Mr. Jacob Macomb and family residing on the South Fork of the Kern, were awakened by the water and had barely time to leave the house before it fell."

Further up the South Fork, the flood waters rousted the Smith family from their home. Thomas Smith, his wife Sophia, their three small children and Mrs. Smith's blind father, were forced to climb a nearby mountainside where they continued upstream to the J. V. Roberts ranch to take refuge.

Along with the debris from destroyed mills and homes, the Keyesville area was littered with

The remains of an old Chinese camp in Keyesville Gulch.

all the remnants of a hard won township and the last signs of the big dream of El Dorado. Many of the discouraged miners left their quartz mines flooded with water and moved on. For the diehard prospectors, the flood had left a new hope. Many new placer deposits had been unearthed by the wild waters of the Kern. They could accept a detour, but not defeat. So they dug themselves out of the mud and started over, true to the miner's code, "maybe . . . tomorrow."

As the flood waters receded, the Chinese miners patiently returned to their placer claims around Keyesville and managed to make a meager living through 1865. In 1979, along Hogeye Creek, there are still small mounds of rocks that mark some of their diggings. There is also a sturdy fireplace, once a part of their settlement, that still stands as mute reminder that the dream of gold challenged men of every race.

Evidence of mining activity in the post-flood era appears regularly in all of the records. In 1862, Joseph Caldwell formed the Cove Mining Company with two men named Oders and Rogers. It would one day be the richest district in the Kern River Valley. The Delonegha Mining District was formed in 1864 and a new rich quartz discovery was made on Clear Creek below Keyesville that led to the formation of the Clear Creek Mining District. In 1865, a twenty-stamp gold mill was built on the Kern River in

Stavert Brothers ready for another day of hard labor at the Keyes Mine in 1914. L to R, Tom, George, Maybon, and Henry Stavert.

the Keyesville Mining District, but the great days were over and the mill operated for only a short time.

The two largest quartz lodes in the Keyesville Mining district, the Keyes and the Mammoth Mines, were worked intermittently for the next 85 years.

The Keyes Mine, also known at one time as the Old Pioneer, was highly successful prior to the

Bodfish miners crossing Kern River, 1910, L to R, Fred Fussell, John Ross, Truthful Brown, George Ross, Charlie Fussell, Wes Rhodehamel, Herman Fussell.

floods of 1861-62. Richard Keyes' dreams of wealth faded when he returned to Keyesville after the flood and found his mine caved in, full of water, and his mill hopelessly out of commission.

Keyes returned to northern California and before long he had extended his mining interests into the Grass Valley country. Within a short time, he relinquished all his claims in the Kern River-Keyesville District, and the Keyes Mine was abandoned.

The Keyes remained inoperative until 1894, when it was purchased by Steven Barton. Barton had homesteaded lands in the Hot Springs Valley in 1886, and in 1893 he had laid out the township of Old Isabella. Barton did not work the Keyes himself and there are no records of any production during the time Barton was the owner.

In 1895, T. N. Stebbens of Lake Isabella was listed in the state mineralogist's reports as the owner of the Keyes Mine, but again no record of gold recovery.

In 1914, the Keyes Mining Company owned the controlling interest in the Keyes Mine. John L. Hooper was president, and George Stavert was the superintendent. Stavert and his brothers, Tom and Maybon, worked out a plan to run a drainage tunnel into the mine at a point 350 feet beneath the old Keyes tunnel. They succeeded in removing the water from the mine so that it was once again operative, but the production of gold was far from financially sound.

By 1920, the Keyes was operating on a part time basis under the supervision of A. M. Arnold. Ownership was listed in the name of the Keyes Mining and Milling Company, and ore was being processed in a ten-stamp mill.

In 1929, the Keyes Mine was leased to the National Engineering Company of Anaheim by the Keyes Mining and Milling Company. Charles Randall was the President and Herbert Lee was superintendent. There were six employees and several new shafts were worked to a depth of 450 feet. The average gold recovery was $100 per ton. From one single extraction of 100 tons of ore, $84 in gold was recovered from the plates. The equipment being used included a pneumatic compressor that operated four drills; a five-stamp mill with 1,100 pound stamps; two concentrators and amalgamation plates. The plant was powered by a 25 h.p. gas engine.

By 1932, the reported total amount of production from the Keyes was $450,000. The Keyes differed from other quartz veins in the district because all of the gold had been taken out by way of a single tunnel which was about 2,100 feet long.

In 1933, the Keyes Mine was owned by Albert Cash, head of the Kern River Mining Company. The Keyes Mines were composed of thirteen claims totaling 360 acres. Cash leased the mine to several men in the next few years, hoping that Keyesville's first mine could be returned to peak production. Some of the foremen during that time were Jerry Sanders, Al Martinez, John and George Ross, and Barney Gordon. The average product was about $40 gold per ton. In 1933, 52 tons of quartz ore was mined from the 100-foot level and paid $39.50 gold per ton.

From 1935 to 1948, Mr. and Mrs.John Howard Copelin lived on the Keyes claim as overseers. The last prospector to lease the mine and gamble on its production possibilities was C. B. Swift. His modern methods and improvements cost him $15,000, and the most he ever took out in gold was about $1500.

In 1948, John and Ivie Copelin purchased the Keyes Mine from Albert Cash and continued to work it on a moderate scale. The mine never again gave up its riches as it had to Richard Keyes, but it has remained a famous first in the mining history of the Kern River District. Over a period of 68 years it produced $450,000 in gold.

The Mammoth Mine is probably the best known of the claims in the Keyesville Mining District. It had a long list of owners and a history of producing in the most on-again-off-again manner that completely baffled the early owners. Even the most experienced prospectors and hard rock experts were unable to figure out the "disappearing vein."

The early miners were constantly faced with the question of what was the best method of extracting the gold from quartz ore. In time, the heavy stamps were only used to crush the ore; gold was recovered most successfully by running the ore sands over copper plates that had been rubbed with mercury. The plates were on "shaker tables" placed below the crushers. The tables agitated and left the gold particles adhered to the mercury. The plates were scraped off at regular intervals and the pulp removed for further amalgamation treatment.

Tom Stavert and his arrastra at the Keyes Mine.

In 1859, Abia T. Lightner was the owner of the Mammoth Mine. It had ceased to produce any gold at all, so Lightner sold the mine to Redfield and Company. After some time the vein was once again found and worked and the Mammoth operated with moderate success.

In 1888, Judge Joseph W. Sumner owned the Mammoth Mine and the only stamp mill on the Kern River, and also was operating several water-powered arrastras. At this time the Mammoth vein had been worked to a depth of 75 feet for a distance of nearly 800 feet along the vein.

In 1896, the Mammoth was owned by Fred Tibbetts and was known as the Harrison Mine. It now embraced four claims — the Mammoth, the Little Mammoth, the Burdette, and the Tom Lane. Though the mine had once again been idle for a period of years, Tibbetts began working it by using a series of tunnels along the vein.

The last quartz mill was built on the Kern River about 1896, just below Keyesville. It was a

Keyes Mill — 1979. Remains of the 10-stamp mill erected at the Keyes Mill by John Hooper in 1915. Stamps are still intact at rear. The left hand table was used to separate gold from crushed ore.

Joseph Warren Sumner

Mr. Pickering, the millman, inside Mammoth Mill, 1910.

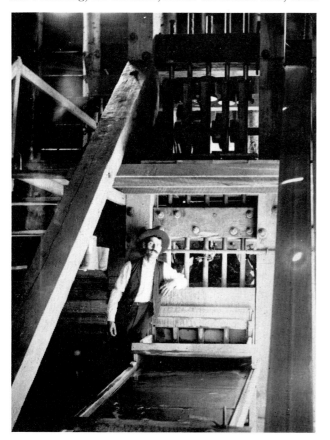

ten-stamp mill run by water power. Though it had originally been built to mill the quartz rock from the Mammoth, the new mill also crushed ore for the smaller mine owners in the area. The millman was named Pickering, and he and his wife lived in Keyesville and ran a boarding house for miners for many years.

In 1904, Frank Howard was the recorded owner of the Mammoth Mine, with the Stavert brothers acting as superintendents. The mine was still producing in good fashion at the turn of the century.

In 1914, The Pacific Light and Power Company obtained the rights to use all of the Kern River waters below old Kernville to power the Borel hydroelectric plant. As part of the agreement, the power company arranged with H. M. Russell, president of the Mammoth Mining Company, new owners of the Mammoth, to move the stamp mill to the mine site and furnish it with electric power. A. G. Keating was production manager of the Mammoth that year, and nine men were employed in the mine. Production was good for the next four years, so Russell sold a part interest in the Mammoth to John and Ivie Copelin, who worked the Mammoth for seventeen years. A description of the ore value and the work being done in the Mammoth was detailed in the 1929 report of the State Mineralogist:

MAMMOTH MINE — It comprises 12 claims, totaling 240 acres, situated in the Keyes Mining District, in Sec. 35, T. 26 S., R. 32 E., M.D.M. 5 miles south of Isabella. Elevation is 3850 feet. Owner, Mammoth Mining Company; J. H. Copelin, President; G. W. Russell, Secretary. Offices: Chamber of Commerce Building, Los Angeles.

The property was discovered in 1855, shortly after the discovery of the Keyes Mine and has been operated off and on for the past sixty years. The property is reported to have a production record of $3,000,000. The Mammoth Vein is from 2 to 15 feet wide, average width being 3 feet.

Mine equipment consists of single drum; 10 h.p. electric-driven hoist; Deming triples pump driven by 3 h.p. motor; 12" by 12" compressor driven by 50 h.p. motor; blacksmith shop and dwellings.

Mill equipment consists of 10-stamp mill, 1000-pound stamps; amalgamation plates. The mill is electrically driven.

The Copelins operated the Mammoth until 1935, when they sold their interest in the mine back to George Russell, and took over the man-

Mammoth Mill 1914.

agement of the Keyes Mine. Russell hired Rosewell Tibbetts as superintedent and put John Luthie in charge of the timbering work in the tunnels. Other local men employed by Russell were Al Martinez, Barney Gordon, and Alvin B. Coe. These were the last great days of the Mammoth Mine.

War was declared in 1941, and by 1942 the effects of World War II had caused a short supply of men, powder, and steel. The government discouraged all mining that was not directly involved with wartime production, and the Mine was closed. Al Coe stayed on the payroll as caretaker, a job he faithfully held until 1969.

The State Mineralogist's report for 1957-58 listed the Mammoth Mine as owned by the Rudnick Estate of Bakersfield. The Mammoth claim was composed of twelve unpatented claims and three millsites. The report stated, "One man is engaged in maintenance and repair work. No production. Mine is idle."

For 27 years, Al never missed a day at the Mammoth. He walked every tunnel, checked the timbers in every shaft, plastered up weak spots along the walls, and replaced light bulbs in the main passages. He wanted everything to be in readiness when the miners came back. He kept a daily ledger of his hours, of every nail he used, every job he did. He also oiled parts, collected picks, shovels, wires, and equipment to be used when the mine opened again.

He hauled his own personal water supply from the spring that ran through the Mammoth, kept his hard hat and extra boots just inside the entrance. He spent a night in each of the many dwellings around the mine to keep prowlers off-guard. He hung clothes on wash lines outside the deserted miner's cabins and kept a small supply of canned food and a book or two in each place, so that they looked lived-in.

He could walk every inch of the hilly Keyesville countryside in the dark, and no one crossed Hogeye Creek or came near the Mammoth Mine without reckoning with Al Coe. People thought he was eccentric, but actually he was just waiting. Waiting for the men to come back, for the Mammoth to start producing again. Year after year he waited.

Al Coe came to the Kern River mines in 1920. He worked in the Keyes Mine, set up the milling equipment at the Sunrise Mine, and in the early '30s he hired on at the Mammoth to repair all the machinery. He was a wizard mechanic, he could fix anything — but his real love was hard-rock mining.

Over the years, he had acquired the rights to five twenty-acre mining claims in Keyesville and bought the quit-claim deeds to two five-acre millsites. While he waited, he worked his claims, placering by simple panning methods when the streams were running. His possessory interest mining taxes were always paid on time, his assessment work completed and carefully itemized, and he continued to add to his acres of

Pipe break at the Mammoth in 1913. The crew gathered for a rest period outside the mill. L to R, Jim Walter, a miner, "Ted" Morgan, blacksmith, hoistman unknown, Andy Robbins, handyman, Mr. Pickering, millman, Rudy, a miner and Victor Flabaht, a miner.

Al Coe, last of the Keyesville miners.

showed them the "glory hole," hundreds of feet up into the mountain, where the last big strike had been made.

"I was there, boys, all of us whoopin' and hollerin, and even cryin'. Oh! It was a sight to behold!"

In 1969, the Bureau of Land Management ordered all unpatented mining claims which were located on public lands to be returned to public domain. Al was fired, the Mammoth boarded up, and within a short time the buildings around the mine were torn down. The waiting was over.

I suppose you could call Al Coe one of the "victims" of the Kern River El Dorado, but he'd never admit that the years were wasted. He always referred to himself as "a gold rush hipster." He has that certain brand of optimism that was built into the gristle of every man who clawed for gold. It wasn't the discovery of gold that kept them going, nor even the dream of a big strike . . . it was the looking, the "game."

It was the mucking and digging till their muscles ached, it was following a new vein or building a bigger mill. The "game" was the stories they swapped, the hard-won rights to a hunk of creek land, the cave-ins and floods, timbering shafts, repairing over-worked machinery, and starting over . . . again and again. A new stake, a new mountain, and a new start.

In 1977, the Western Mining Association met in northern California with nearly 5,000 members in attendance. The Department of Natural Resources in Bakersfield reported that more than 2,000 unpatented gold mining claims are

Pee Wee Oldham as he appeared in 1979 after forty-two years of placer mining on the Kern River. On the right is his good friend Fred Dodds. Photo taken in front of Miracle Hot Springs Store and Post Office.

mining equipment. There were those who called his Keyesville kingdom a "junk yard," but local businessmen considered his signature on a check as good as gold.

Once in a while, he would agree to guide a tour through the mine, usually for children. Once it was for a group of Girl Scouts from Ridgecrest, who smiled at his stories and sent him a stack of "thank you" letters. Another time, he caught four boys nosing around the stamp mill, and after a stern lecture about "private property," he took them inside the mine and explained in great detail about the rigors of quartz mining.

He made them run their hands over the walls in the main shaft and showed them how the miners learned to follow the strata of the rock; he told them of the slow daily progress measured in inches and broken pick-ax handles. Then he registered in Kern County, all showing their annual $100 proof-of-labor statements. Since patented claims on private land are not required to make reports each year, there is no way of telling how many mines are being worked.

The big registry books at the Kern County Court Building are full of names and townships on Greenhorn Mountain and in the Kern River Valley. Names like Burning Moscow, Golden Glow, Eagle, Blue Jay, and Homestake.

On a chilly spring day in 1978, Pee Wee Oldham, 72, gathered his supplies together and prepared to head back to his mining claim, the Broken Hip No. 1, located about five miles downstream from Miracle Hot Springs on the Kern River.

Pee Wee lives on his claim six months of the year till the cold weather "sets his bones to achin'," then he moves to town. He says he is the only miner working a placer claim on the river this year. He has to contend with the rules of the State Bureau of Mines, who monitor his operation. He grumbles about how tough they make it. "No sluices off the bank, have to dig a swing hole to use a long tom because everything has to go back in the river — can't take nothin' out of the river, 'cept the gold!"

Someone in the small group standing around the wizened old miner asks, "Think you'll make a big gold strike this time, Pee Wee?"

The weathered face crinkles up in a grin and his eyes flash with good humor. He takes a long-look at the man who asked the age-old question, then Pee Wee Oldham, who has mined the Kern River since the '30s, answers confidently, "Yup!"

Like the Idler said, ". . . mining has great influence on the feelings and passions of men . . . for they will mine, and continue to mine, so long as the universe holds."

II
The Shootin' Walkers

THE ONLY dwelling that has been preserved from the gold rush days in the Hot Springs Valley is the Old Walker House. Shaded by ancient digger pines, the house stands just south of the site of the old mining town of Keyesville, about 2½ miles west of the junction of Highway 155 and Keyesville Road. It has been in its present location for over 100 years.

The original house was one large room built for the Widow Digman, who cooked meals for the miners who worked in the Mammoth Mine. The room was twenty feet square, with hand-hewn ceilings held in place with square nails, and warmed by a large native rock fireplace.

The house was built on the twenty-acre Brite Spot mining claim, listed as one of the major gold producers in the Keyesville Mining District during the early years.

The Old Walker House is now owned by Faye and Rulon Scott, natives of Utah. They came to Wofford Heights in 1958 and opened a coffee shop where the El Vacquero Restaurant is today. In 1960, Rulon began a sixteen-year career with the Kern Union School District, teaching at Camp Owen in Kernville for thirteen years, then at Kern Valley High School for three years till his retirement.

The Scotts bought the Old Walker House in 1962 from Dean and Lorena Bell, who had lived there since 1932. During their thirty-year residence, the Bells brought the plumbing indoors and added the bathroom.

The house now has four rooms and a bath, the original room is the Scotts' living room on the north side of the building and the century-old ceilings are as sturdy in 1979 as they were in Widow Digman's day.

In the process of renovating the kitchen, the Scotts found that the walls had once been covered with layers of newspapers dated in 1896. That was probably the year that the 9 by 18 foot room was added. In tracing the former owners of the house, Rulon Scott names three families who occupied the Old Walker House prior to 1932: the Baileys, the Marshalls, and Mary Walker Stavert's family.

The Walker family, who are the central characters of the legend you are about to read, did not live in the Old Walker House until the 1880's, but members of the family had lived in Hot Springs Valley since the 1860's.

William Brannon Walker, Sr., was the patriarch of the local clan. He was born in Georgia and crossed the plains in a covered wagon from Texas during the years of the western migration. William and his teen-age bride, Mary, tried their luck in the northern California gold fields and moved about from one mining community to another. Two of their eight children, Tom and Jim, were born during those early nomadic years.

In the 1860's, William and Mary and their two sons settled in the Keyesville area. Mary bore five more sons — Ben, Hal, Newt, Phil, Bill Jr., and one daughter, Mary.

As the Walker boys grew to manhood, they all became proficient with a gun. Each of them killed at least one man during his lifetime, with the exception of Bill Jr. The times were violent, and guns were a way of life — a "fast draw" made a hero of many a cowboy. Whatever the circumstances were that led the Walker men to kill, they always had one champion — their father, William Sr. He once made the remark, "My boys have all got their man, but Bill, and he'll get his yet!"

Old Walker House as it looked in 1924.

Tom, the eldest, got his first man in Kernville. Shot him right between the eyes. He killed his second man in Arizona. He was convicted of murder and spent ten years in the dungeons of Yuma Prison. He was considered the best shot of all the Walker men, and in fast draw second only to Newt. After serving a long sentence for the Arizona murder, Tom returned to the Hot Springs Valley to mine with his brothers.

Jim Walker was born in Placer County, California, and came to the Kern River mines with his parents when he was very young. He worked at a variety of jobs in the valley throughout his life, and never left his Hot Springs home except for one wild fling in San Francisco. His excursion to the big city ended abruptly when he was roughly awakened from a drugged slumber and found he had been shanghaied and was on board a ship headed for South America. The tale of his escape made a riotous campfire story for a long time after he returned to the Kern River.

Jim was known to act impulsively, and two of

the notches on his gun bear out that notion. In 1904, he was working as a blacksmith on the Borel Canal construction crew, and living in a tent on the site. He awoke one morning just in time to see a Mexican worker leaving his tent under rather suspicious circumstances, so Jim grabbed his gun and shot the man. The court judged it justifiable homicide.

The second incident happened in Old Isabella. Jim and an Indian from the South Fork were drinking together in the saloon one night, getting drunker as the hours passed by. When the bar closed, the two got another bottle of whiskey, settled down under the bridge north of town, and proceeded to finish it off. They both fell asleep and slept heavily into the early morning. It just so happened that Bill Walker, Jim's younger brother, rode by the bridge on his way to Kernville that morning and saw Jim and the Indian dead to the world.

Bill knew that Jim had been carrying a lot of money the night before, so he went down to his

Jim Walker

– Ardis Walker photo.

brother and, after failing to wake him, Bill took Jim's wallet for safekeeping so that nobody would rob him while he was passed out.

When Jim finally came to, he was groggy and still half drunk. He remembered the money he'd had with him the night before, and fumbled around looking for his wallet. When he discovered it was gone, he pulled his gun and killed the Indian. He made a simple deduction — the money was gone and there were only two of them there. The next day, Bill returned the wallet to Jim and explained why he had taken it. Jim just shook his head in disbelief, "H —, I just killed a man for that!"

Sometime after the 1880's, a feud began which involved three families — the Walkers, the Gibsons, and the Burtons. It rivaled the Kentucky feud of the Hatfields and the McCoys, and then some.

The cast of characters in the three-family feud was sizeable. There were the seven Walker brothers; two Gibson brothers — Bert and Bill; and four Burton brothers — Jim, Fletcher, Dave, and Luther.

All the boys of the families had grown up together in Hot Springs Valley, working and fishing and hunting together. From all accounts they got along well, were popular, and considered hard workers.

In the 1880's Jack Spratt entered the picture. Spratt, a resident of the Indian Wells Valley, and his Indian wife lived in Grapevine Canyon on the Mojave Desert. Spratt sported a bushy red beard which made him less than anonymous on more than one occasion.

A case in point: a lady traveling to Lone Pine by stage was among the unlucky occupants to be robbed by a lone bandit, whose red beard was not well concealed. On the return trip, the stage was stopped again by the same bandit, and the passengers were relieved of their valuables. The exasperated lady, who recognized the bushy red beard of the highwayman, reportedly exclaimed, "Mr. Spratt, this isn't fair! You robbed me on the way up, and now on the way back, too."

Despite Spratt's bad reputation, he was a likeable fellow and he was on friendly terms with both the Walkers and the Burtons. Reports of the hold-up of the Kernville stage between Havilah and Hot Springs Valley brought suspicion on Fletcher and Jim Burton when the empty Wells Fargo box was discovered at the Burton mill on Clear Creek.

The Burton boys, still in their teens, blew the whistle on Jack Spratt. He was sentenced to a long stay in San Quentin and, before he was taken away, he vowed that he would get even with the Burtons.

The Walker boys evidently felt that Spratt had been framed by the Burtons, and a coolness developed between the families. This initial strain on their friendship was further aggravated by a mining dispute. It seemed that all three families claimed rights to a mine near Keyesville. Jim and Fletcher Burton made it known that they intended to work the mine, regardless of all the Walkers or Gibsons who walked the face of the earth.

The Gibson brothers had a ranch in Hot Springs Valley and before the feud erupted, their sister, Adie, married Dave Burton. The marriage made allies of the Gibsons and the Burtons, whether they were willing or not.

By 1891, all three families were mining in the Keyesville area, the muttered threats intensified, and everyone was going around armed to the teeth. The time for talk had passed.

One wintery night, Jim Burton left the cabin he shared with his brother, Fletcher, and went to Kernville for supplies. While Fletcher was working around the cabin, a sudden blast left him sprawled on the cabin floor. That same night, Jim was cut down by shots fired through the window of the bar where he was having a drink. Jim was badly wounded, but he survived. Fletcher was dead.

The chief suspect was Jack Spratt, who had recently been released from prison, and was reported to be in the valley. However, it was proven that Spratt had been in the Mojave Desert at the time of the shootings. Authorities then turned their attentions to the Gibson brothers, who had made numerous loud threats against the Burtons. The Gibsons were unable to come up with a satisfactory alibi for the night of the shootings, so they were arrested and taken to the Bakersfield jail to await trial.

Sometime during the long trial, Ben Walker disappeared from his home; headed into Indian territory. No importance was placed on this event during the trial, but Ben was never heard from again.

Witnesses, including Charlie Allison, a neighbor of the Gibsons and a partner in previous mining ventures, loudly proclaimed their innocence throughout the trial, but the brothers were convicted of first degree murder on circumstantial evidence, and sentenced to life imprisonment in San Quentin.

Jim Burton recovered from his wounds, but further trouble was still brewing in the Keyesville hills. Charlie Allison continued to insist that his former partners were innocent and, whenever he and Jim Burton happened to meet, violence threatened to explode.

Whether by chance or by formal agreement, the two met on the trail just before it crossed the footbridge below Keyesville. A miner, who had stopped to rest nearby, watched as Allison and Burton circled each other warily, each looking for an opening. The miner reported that he heard a pistol shot echo against the hills, and Jim Burton lay dead.

Allison was tried, but his plea of self-defense was accepted by the jury, and he was acquitted.

With the two older Burtons dead, the mantle of the family passed on to the two surviving

L to R, Will and Charlie Gibson, Dolly and Ben Burton, children of Dave Burton in Old Kernville.

brothers, Dave and Luther, and the feud raged on.

Over the years, the cause of the Gibson boys attracted serious attention. A petition signed by jury members, county officials, and prominent citizens brought about a review of the evidence used to convict them, and the fact of Ben Walker's strange disappearance. A plea was made to the parole board and, after reconsidering all the elements in the case, the Gibson brothers were set free.

On October 7, 1904, the Walkers were in the news again. This time it was Phil Walker, charged with the murder of Bill Nicoll. Nicoll had been drinking pretty heavily in a saloon on the Kernville — Havilah Road. He told those within earshot that he was on his way to Bakersfield to buy farm machinery. Phil Walker, Pat Palmer, Anastasia Urdangarian, a Mexican employed on the Palmer Ranch, and Antonio Suniga, an Indian, decided to relieve Nicoll of his cash. Nicoll put up a struggle, and Phil hit him over the head with a piece of pipe to persuade him to cooperate. The blow resulted in Nicoll's death.

The four men appeared before Superior Court Judge Bennett in April, 1905. Palmer turned state's evidence and named Walker as the one who had wielded the murder weapon. Walker was found guilty, and sentenced to life imprisonment in San Quentin.

William Walker and his son, Newt, attended the trial in Bakersfield on Saturday. Early on

Phil Walker

Monday they were returning to Keyesville, when the next chapter of the Walker-Burton feud started. The two men had taken the Petersen Stage from Caliente to Havilah, the half-way point between the rail head at Caliente and Keyesville. They got off in Havilah to have lunch and within minutes Newt had killed two men, Dave Burton and George Bagsby.

The account of the events that followed the shooting was not made clear for some time, since the two Bakersfield papers, the *Daily Californian*, and the *Bakersfield Echo*, carried conflicting stories.

The first articles appeared in the *Daily Californian* on April 25, 1905. It stated that Burton and Bagsby were walking down the street in Havilah. When they were opposite Gus Miller's store, Newt Walker came to the door, saw his ancient enemy, then stepped out onto the porch and started shooting. Burton was not carrying a gun, but Bagsby had a pistol, and returned fire. Walker fired six times, two bullets hit Burton and three struck Bagsby. Newt left the two men dead

in the street and left on foot in the direction of Kernville.

That early account of the shooting made Newt Walker out to be a cold blooded gunman. It also missed a few facts.

Deputy Gonzales in Kernville was notified and came straight to Havilah, but he did not pass Newt on the way. It was common knowledge that there was an arsenal of weapons in the Walker cabin at Keyesville. Authorities agreed that if Newt reached the cabin he would be well-armed and would probably put up a desperate fight if deputies tried to arrest him.

Other officers arriving from Bakersfield in Havilah after the shooting were Deputy Sheriff Joe DeMara, Sheriff Kelly, and Coroner Mullins.

Despite the wild stories of the cold-blooded killer, Newt Walker surrendered himself to the sheriff in Isabella. Joe Ferris, Newt's mining partner, met with Sheriff Kelly and Constable Johnnie Swett in Old Isabella and told them that Newt was in the hills and was prepared to give himself up. He did just that at 8 p.m. on April 25.

The autopsy, performed by Dr. Newberry, revealed that all but one wound was fatal. Burton received two bullets through his body within inches of each other. Bagsby was also shot twice through the body; a third shot inflicted a flesh wound in Bagsby's hip. The two body shots were within two inches of each other, both were fatal.

Walker's trial began on June 13, 1905 and he was tried first for the Burton killing. The big stumbling block to the defense plea of justifiable homicide was the fact that Dave Burton was unarmed at the time he was shot. The defense produced two witnesses to testify that Newt Walker had reason to believe that Burton was armed.

The first witness was William Yates. He testified that he had seen Burton and Bagsby in A. Brown's store in Havilah that day after the stage had arrived. Yates stated that the two men were talking and Burton held and patted a pistol in his hand.

Ephraim Williams, a miner who lived in Havilah, was the second witness. He testified that he had seen Burton and Bagsby just a few minutes before they entered Miller's store and that Burton had a pistol in his hip pocket. It seemed reasonable to assume that Burton had given the pistol to Bagsby prior to entering the store, a fact which Walker could not have known.

Walker testified that he had seen Burton and

Bagsby in front of Dooley's Saloon just after they got off the stage, and at that time Burton had a gun in his hip pocket. He said he and his father went on over to Miller's store. His testimony continued, "We went into Miller's, my father and I, and bought a can of sardines and some crackers to make a light lunch. We had paid our fare to Havilah and expected to walk on to Keyesville. While we were sitting down eating, Bagsby and Burton passed by the door. They saw us and came inside. They walked around the room, making remarks to each other, Burton to the effect that the Burtons always came out on top and he wasn't afraid of anybody. I asked if that remark was meant for me, and he said I could take it as I pleased.

"My father said that we did not want any trouble and that we had better go, so we went out into the street. Burton said, 'What was that remark you made? We had started up the road and they were apparently following us. I looked back over my shoulder. I saw Bagsby with his hand on his pistol, the weapon being in his pocket. I started walking again and Bagsby said, 'Hold on, we want you.'

"I turned again and Burton then put his hand towards his hip pocket. When I wheeled around and began to fire, my recollection is that I shot Bagsby first. I thought I was going to be shot down right there and then."

Even when subjected to stiff cross examination, Newt steadfastly stuck to his story. The prosecution kept coming back to the fact that it seemed impossible that Walker was able to draw and kill two men after Bagsby had started his draw and Dave Burton had reached for his hip pocket.

Determined to break down Newt's story, the district attorney asked Newt to demonstrate his actions on the fateful day. Newt put on his gun and holster while Emmons, the attorney representing Bagsby looked on.

One story reported that Newt called to Judge Mahon to take out his handkerchief and before the judge could do so, Newt had drawn his pistol on Emmons and clicked the hammer four times. When Newt Walker left the stand after that demonstration of his incredible speed with a gun, everyone in court was a believer in Walker's fast draw.

As the trial progressed, the defense produced a succession of witnesses who testified that Bur-

– Ardis Walker photo.

Newt Walker — fast draw artist.

ton and Bagsby were the aggressors. Joe Gonzales of Kernville testified that Dave Burton had offered him $200 to kill Walker two years earlier. Charlie Tibbetts stated that Bagsby had told him that Dave Burton had brought him (Bagsby) to the area in March for the purpose of killing Newt Walker. Tibbetts said that Bagsby twirled his pistol on his finger the whole time he spoke.

When the defense rested, it was the prosecution's turn.

G. L. Sanders, Special Prosecutor, had been brought in from Los Angeles to try the case against Newt. The *Daily Californian* dubbed Sanders — "Actor-Orator." The Los Angeles attorney seemed a bit flamboyant for Bakersfield courts. A reporter wrote, "He has a pleasing manner, a ready flow of word paintings, but coupled with all this are the traits more ordinarily seen before the footlights than in front of a jury in a court of justice. Sanders acted out every aspect of the case vividly. He pictured the villainous Walker holding up the stagecoach, which in reality had never been held up. Walker, according to Sanders, "was like a leopard whelp who had tasted human blood, had been cheated of his game in the stagecoach incident, and so because of this, had planned to shoot down his enemies in cold blood in Havilah that day."

Sanders strutted in front of the jury box and bellowed, "Why did this murderer run away? Why but for the same reason that Cain, when he felled his brother, hid himself in the hills of Nod and for the same reason that every murderer from the first shedding of human blood by primeval man down to this day has felt his guilt upon him and run from the scene of the crime."

Sanders' oratory ran the gamut of human emotions. The Burton women lifted their veils to dab at their eyes. The Walkers watched grimly as the attorney paced and raved and tried with all his eloquence to put the noose around Newt's neck.

On the final day of the trial, both sides summed up their cases. According to news reports, the defense delivered one of the most elaborate and logical arguments heard in local courts in many a day. They accused Sanders of making far-fetched deductions and factually established that Walker had acted in self defense.

The prosecution declared that murder had been done, even though it seemed that the men met by pure chance. Walker's shooting of the two victims was not justified and thereby inexcusable.

The jury deliberated for four hours and handed down a verdict of "Not Guilty."

Walker was also scheduled to be tried for the Bagsby shooting, but once the jury acquitted him of shooting the unarmed Burton, the district attorney decided he could hardly hope for a conviction for shooting an armed man who fired back at his killer. The Bagsby-Walker case was dismissed.

Newt Walker was a free man again. He returned to Keyesville and managed to stay out of trouble until the summer of 1924. On that occasion, Mike Carrol and Floyd Fischer of Kernville paid a visit to Newt and Tom Walker in Keyesville. The four men decided to drive into old Isabella in Fischer's car. On the way, the car bogged down in the deep sand in French Gulch.

Tom Walker and Mike Carrol decided to go for help in Isabella, and left Newt and Floyd with the car. They alternated digging the car out, with drinking from a jug of whiskey, until an argument broke out. No one knows what Newt and Floyd fought about, but the fact that Floyd Fischer was the son-in-law of Dave Burton whom Newt killed twenty years earlier, may have been part of it. Fischer was shot twice. Even though he was not killed, a warrant was sworn out for Newt, charging him with attempted murder.

Deputy Pat Davis went after Newt, but before he approached the house, he hung his gun on the limb of a tree. After his performance in court during the Bagsby-Burton trial, Newt had been called "Dead Eye."

Newt was sitting on the porch of the Old Walker House when Davis walked up and told him he was wanted for murder. "Where's your gun?" Walker said, "You know you can't take me without a gun." Davis replied, "I know I can't take you *with* one." Newt told Davis to go on to town and tell Sheriff Cas Walser that he would come in the next day. Newt went to trial, and once again the jury brought in a verdict of "Not Guilty."

Four months later, the murder of four miners in the Keyesville hills made banner headlines. One of the dead men was Newt Walker.

On Tuesday morning, November 25, 1924, Mr. and Mrs. Walter Armstrong went up to Keyesville from Old Isabella to get some mining information from Newt Walker. Newt had been sharing his two-room home, the Old Walker House, with two friends, Frank Murdock and Alphonse (Tex) Roland. There was no answer when Armstrong knocked on the front door, so he went around to the back of the house.

Murdock was lying near the woodpile. At first, the Armstrongs thought he was drunk, but closer inspection showed that he was very dead. Newt Walker was lying near the back door of the kitchen, a bullet through his heart. Inside the kitchen, the table was overturned and cards and money were scattered about. The Armstrongs hot-footed it back to town and contacted A. O. "Gus" Suhre, the constable, at his store.

Gus called the sheriff in Kernville to report the killings, and then cranked up his old Chandler and went to Keyesville to investigate. Murdock had been shot through the forehead, besides being dealt a heavy blow with a blunt instrument. Inside the house, Gus found Newt's two pistols lying on his unmade bed, and his rifle leaning against the wall. Gus knew Tex Roland had been living there, but he was nowhere to be found, so Gus went back to Isabella to wait for the authorities.

The officers arrived about dark from Bakersfield. The only road into the valley was through Caliente and Havilah, and it was none too good in those days. Those who came were the Coroner, Norman House; his reporter, Bill Golding, Deputy Sheriff Phil Fickert, and *Bakersfield Californian* cub reporter, Jim Day.

Though it was getting too dark to do much, the men went to Keyesville, and looked around the Old Walker House. They found an empty .38 revolver about 20 feet from Murdock's body, and noted that all of Tex Roland's clothes and personal possessions were gone from the house. Since there was no trace of Tex, the officers feared he might have also killed Tom before taking off. Somehow they learned that Tom Walker had spent that Saturday evening playing cards with Newt, Tex, and Frank. Tom's cabin, which was a short way up the hill, was empty, and no one remembered seeing him in town.

A posse of local men gathered, including Newt's brothers, Phil, Jim, and Bill Jr. They decided on a plan of action for the next morning, and then retired for the night. In the middle of the night, the men were startled from their sleep by the sound of a shot ringing out in the canyon, followed by a piercing, eerie cry. They made an effort to locate the source of the cry and the shot, but darkness forced them to abandon the search till daylight.

The next morning, they enlisted the help of Charlie Woodard, who was considered one of the best trackers in the valley, to help the posse search for the killers. They found tracks that left from Tom Walker's cabin to a deserted mine tunnel a short way up the hill. The tracks went in, but none came out. Phil Walker and Deputy Phil Fickert crept into the tunnel and found Tom Walker's body slumped against a side wall. There was a pistol in his hand, and a bullet hole in his head. He had shot himself. Nearby were two empty bottles that had contained moonshine whiskey. When they got Tom's body out of the tunnel, they found he was wearing Tex's shoes. The next day, the *Bakersfield Californian*

Tom Walker — He never missed.

declared, "Find Tex, dead or alive, and the mystery is solved."

On Friday, the three men were buried. Eighteen friends and neighbors carried the caskets about 300 feet up the trail in back of the Old Walker House to an oak-shaded knoll. There was no room in the small fenced cemetery plot started seventy years earlier by the Lightner family, so the three men were buried just south of the plot. There were no flowers, no music, and no elaborate service. Friends silently paid their last respects to these men who had died as violently as they lived.

Bill Nestell had walked to the funeral site from his home in Keyesville, and after the service was over, he headed home by way of a shortcut through the gulch just below the cemetery. It was in that gulch that he discovered the body of Tex Roland. He had been shot several times. Nearby was a bloody wheelbarrow that had been used to transport the body to a shallow mine shaft in the gulch. In the days that followed, men who

39

had known the Walkers remembered that Newt Walker had taken pride in his skill with a gun, that the only man he feared and he knew could outdraw him was his brother, Tom Walker. The last chapter of the Walker-Burton feud had been written.

Bill Walker Jr. remained the only one of the family that did not "get his man." He kept his gun holstered. Haunted, perhaps, by the senseless, violent deaths of his brothers.

Bill Jr. and his wife, Etta, had four children — Frank, William, Ardis and Berniece. Bill struggled to wrest a living from the old Keyesville mine for many years, even after Etta decided to leave the dreary, nearly deserted town of Keyesville and moved to Fresno with the children, where she opened a boardinghouse.

To date, six generations of the Walker family have lived in the Kern River Valley. Most familiar to valley residents is Ardis Walker, who will long be remembered for his many contributions to the Kern River Valley.

Ardis Manley Walker was born in Keyesville in 1901. As a youngster, he walked ten miles each day via the old footbridge below the Mammoth Mine to attend school in Old Isabella. Later, he graduated from high school in Fresno and attended Fresno State College for a while. He earned a degree in Electrical Engineering from the University of Southern California and was subsequently hired by Bell Telephone Company to work in their New York offices.

Manhattan was a fascinating place for a young man who had grown up in the Sierra Nevada mountains, but his heart remained in the vaulting, granite canyons of Keyesville, and the high country wilderness above the Kern River. His memories of his birthplace inspired his earliest writings, and first book of poetry, *Quatrains*, was published during the time he worked in New York.

The Depression left New York stunned and ugly with disillusion and panic. Ardis decided to give up his job and city life and he returned to his Keyesville home.

He worked a mining claim in La Mismo Gulch during the daylight hours, and at night he continued writing. He took a job with the *Bakersfield Californian* as a correspondent, and was a stringer for the AP wire services. During the next few years, he mined less and less, and devoted most of his time to writing.

Ardis M. Walker

In 1937, he met and married a petite schoolteacher, Gayle Mendelssohn, and for practical reasons returned to mining briefly, operating the stamp mill at the Keyes Mine.

In 1938, he was elected to the First District Judicial Court, and served on the Isabella bench until 1948. Politics was a "natural" for Ardis, and he campaigned successfully for the office of First District Supervisor. He thundered about in county politics for four years, defending local projects in his district, and good government in general.

With the completion of the Isabella Dam and Reservoir in 1953, Ardis turned his energies toward developing recreational possibilities of the Kern River Valley. He owned and operated a motel in Kernville for eleven years, and was active in all the civic affairs until he retired in 1964.

In the next years he published several books including: *The Sierra Prologue, Sierra Sequence, Francisco Garces, The Rough and the Righteous,* and wrote the verse for *Haiku* and *Camera* in collaboration with the local photographer, Bob Luthey.

Ardis helped to organize the Kern Plateau Association, which directs its efforts towards protecting the natural habitat of the native Golden Trout at the headwaters of the Kern River. A devout conservationist, Ardis has fought to keep his native land from being destroyed by the increasing demands of recreationists.

Through his writing, Ardis has recorded his memories of the Walker family as one of the pioneer families in the Hot Springs Valley. There was laughter as well as violence in those early years, and history must record it all.

III

The Great Circuit

A S SURELY as the appearance of wildflowers on the hillsides around the Kern River Valley heralded the arrival of spring, so the season was also announced by the bands of sheep bleating along the dusty roads on their annual trek from the San Joaquin Valley to the Mojave Desert and the high country pastures.

The sheep industry in California, which has not only clothed the population but fed them as well, dates back more than 200 years. Beginning with only a few small bands of sheep, by 1825 there were an estimated two million head of sheep in the state. One million head were privately owned, another one million head were quartered at many Franciscan missions located throughout California.

The chain of missions had been established by Father Junipero Serra, the first one in 1769. Educated in Mexico, Father Serra spent most of his life journeying about the countryside, on foot, preaching to people in remote areas. The first sheep may have been brought from Mexico into California during his travels. The Mexican breed was very coarse-wooled and was raised primarily for meat. The primitive missions provided enough land for the sheep to graze and the limited amount of tending necessary.

By the turn of the century, there were many independent flocks, and sheepmen who were looking for ways to raise a finer wool breed. Of the early ranches, the Rancho El Tejon was one of the largest, with 100,000 ewes. The Miller and Lux Ranch, established in 1858, ran between 80,000 and 100,000 ewes. They eventually ran some 200,000 head of sheep, and bought an additional 80,000 ewes each year to feed.

The Kern County sheep industry began to make real strides in 1860, when Solomon W. Jewett drove a band of fine-wooled imported French Merino sheep all the way from Vermont into what would one day be Kern County. Jewett is credited with being instrumental in helping to establish nearly all of the California flocks of Merino sheep.

The French Merino is directly descended from the Spanish Merino breed. The Spanish government jealously guarded their prized breed, but did little to improve them. Some crafty, western-styled rustlers smuggled some of the sheep out of Spain and into France, Germany, and England, where the breed was highly improved. Today, the American Merino is considered the best in the world, and there are more sheep with Merino blood than any other breed. A Merino ram will yield up to 28 pounds of wool at shearing, enough for eight men's suits.

Sheepmen had two ways to raise their animals. On the range, which was the most important and practical method; or on a ranch, which required quantities of hay and grain. The early country around the San Joaquin Valley was sparsely populated, and the range lands were plentiful. The desert and the mountains provided all the year-round grazing country that sheepmen needed. They ranged bands of sheep for at least ten months of the year, taking them from the San Joaquin Valley on the "great circuit," around the desert, through the mountains, across the Kern Plateau and down several pre-selected routes into Visalia. Some ranchers rented out their fields to the sheepmen, and the sheep ate the second crop of grape leaves after they returned from the circuit. They stayed in ranch headquarters for about two months, and then began the circuit all over again.

All Kern County sheep business revolved around the annual "great circuit" drive. Beginning in the early spring, the sheep were moved from winter quarters in bands of 2,000-2,500. Sheepherders used a number of different routes to reach mountain pasture lands, but the two main sheep driveways were referred to as the Tehachapi Driveway and the Greenhorn Driveway.

Most sheepmen preferred the Tehachapi route, particularly those whose home ranches were centered in the Delano area. The trail led in a southeasterly direction from the San Joaquin Valley to Comanche Point, through the Cummings Valley, then east through Tehachapi and over the mountain ranges to the Mojave Desert. Once on the desert ranges, the band traveled north along the foothills to Sand Canyon or Nine Mile Canyon, then west onto the Kern Plateau, where they fed in all the lush high country meadows, including Chimney Meadow, Kennedy Meadows, and Monache Meadow.

The last portion of the "great circuit" led the herders onto the Deer Mountain range and north through pasture lands such as those belonging to the A. Brown Co., then west across the Kern River, over the Great Western Divide, down the Kaweah River watershed and into Visalia, or south to Delano.

The Greenhorn Driveway, which led through Hot Springs Valley, usually originated at Granite Station, where the sheep were sheared to relieve them of their heavy coats before heading for the long circuit journey. Traveling east, the herders drove the sheep through Poso Flat and over the old Greenhorn Trail. They crossed the Kern River near Isabella, then moved east through the South Fork Valley, over Walker's Pass and onto the Mojave Desert. Feed was considered very good on the desert route and bands often moved north as far as Lone Pine before turning west over Cottonwood Pass and south onto the Kern Plateau. They fed through the meadows as they moved west, using the same river crossing as the Tehachapi herds, crossing the Great Western Divide, and following the Kaweah River trail into Visalia.

A very rough estimate of the mileage covered during the circuit drive is about 600 miles. Herders were evidently well prepared to take sheep wherever there was feed, and to tackle any kind of weather or emergency they encountered during the long months of the drive.

It took men of great physical stamina to follow the rugged, nomadic life of a herder. Most of the

Sheep going east on Highway 178 past the A. Brown Ranch in Weldon.

herders had served their apprenticeships in the sheep business as young boys. Many came to America from Spain and France, but it was the Basque sheepmen from the Pyrenees Mountains of Europe that settled in large numbers in Kern County. They began migrating to California in the 1870's and some of their descendants are still in the sheep business today.

Among the young Basque sheepherders who came to Kern County in 1872 was Faustino Noriega. After a three-month voyage around Cape Horn, he had arrived in San Francisco and taken the railroad to the end of the tracks in Delano. He walked from there into Bakersfield. Faustino had no sponsor to help him, and he spoke no English, but he knew his trade and he was eager to work. He was sheep boss for the Miller and Lux Ranch for many years, and established himself as one of the most knowledgeable sheepmen in the county. His son, Albert, carried on the family name in the sheep industry and another son, Frank, is a well-known Kern County judge.

Faustino, and the other young herders who arrived in those early years, had worked with sheep in the wilds of the Pyrenees Mountains. Their experiences had developed the physical and mental training so necessary to men who spent months on the trail, away from family and civilization. They were in great demand by the local sheep owners, who needed trustworthy herders to take the responsibility for hundreds of animals on the long circuit drive.

Sheep going through Old Isabella towards Walker's Pass.

Most sheepmen, particularly those driving their bands over the Greenhorn Driveway, had their sheep sheared before starting over the mountains or through the desert. Granite Station became a major shearing center when Leopold Vignave bought the stage stop in 1883. He built shearing sheds and long watering troughs for the sheep, and a dining hall, barroom, stable and hotel for the herders. Leopold did a thriving business for many years.

At shearing time, the herders, shearers, the freighters who hauled the wool to the railroad at Delano, and the wool buyers, formed quite a group. At the height of the shearing season, they were joined by professional gamblers who followed the shearing camps to fleece the sheep shearers.

Guy Hughes, who recorded the early days of Granite Station, recalled that shearing time was a wild and colorful time. Though he was just a young boy, Hughes remembered the flurry of activity in the shearing sheds, and one particular paymaster, Robert Gilliam, who made an indelible impression on him.

Gilliam, a seasonal paymaster for the sheepmen, sat at the cashier's desk with a wool sack that hung on a rack. As each shearer finished a sheep, he would throw the fleece into the wool sack and receive a five cent piece from the pile of coins Gilliam had piled on the desk in front of him. A good shearer clipped the fleece off in one piece. Bat Albitre was one of the top shearers and, on a good day, he made about $2.50, which meant he sheared 50 sheep with hand clippers.

The Indian shearers were good at their work, but their heavy losses at poker and the Granite Station whiskey left them broke and mean. They would snip at Gilliam with their shears in an effort to get more nickels, but Gilliam was ready for them. With a husky wagon spoke in his left hand, he would calmly bat an over-zealous Indian over the head, and with his right hand he continued to hand out nickels as business went on as usual.

Once the shearing was over, and the wool sold and hauled away, the herders left the poker tables and the bars and the company of friends, and began the long drive over the great circuit.

Two herders were usually in charge of a band of 2,000-2,500 sheep. Since sheep tend to stay close together, they could be handled with a minimum of labor. The herder's most valuable assistants were sheep dogs. The sheep dog was a special breed developed over the years to watch and herd the sheep, and to ward off predators. The sheep dog was most often a Border Collie or Australian Shepherd, or a mixture of both breeds. Loyal and intelligent, these dogs were the only companions the herders had during the long months on the trail. Herders stayed with the sheep 24 hours a day and seven days a week. The dogs were on duty for the same amount of time. Days off came only when the bands were safely back in winter headquarters.

The herders drove their sheep slowly across the ranges, allowing them plenty of time to graze if feed was plentiful, picking up the pace only if the range feed was sparse. The Mojave Desert was considered excellent range in the early days since the sheep liked to eat all the little woods and shrubs and could travel for long periods without water. Later on, government regulations required the band to move at least five miles a day.

The herders had few needs. All their gear was packed on the backs of several well-trained burros, who stayed with the sheep during the day. Sometimes, if they were in an accessible area, a "camp tender," driving a team and spring wagon, would meet the herders with supplies, but most of the time, the two men were on their own.

At night, the burros were unpacked and relieved of the few items of camp gear, which included a bed roll and cooking utensils. They carried a small tent to use in bad weather, but most of the nights were spent in the open, under the stars. Their cooking utensils were an iron pot, an iron kettle, a Dutch oven, and a few tools to cook and eat with. The food was simple fare —

A band of sheep file past the Hot Springs House.

mutton or lamb, a few onions and potatoes, sourdough bread baked in the Dutch oven, cheese made with sheep's milk, and plenty of hearty Basque wine. Many herders substituted wine for water during the day. Perhaps, wine helped to pass the long days and weeks in a more pleasant frame of mind.

Once the sheep had grazed the desert and the foothills, they moved into the high country meadows. It is nearly impossible to establish a date when sheep first began to use the high Sierras since few records were kept before 1850. Dates carved on trees in different areas of the high country indicate that bands of sheep from valley missions grazed there during drought years in the late 1700's.

Signs of sheep driveways and herders' camps were found as early as 1870 by South Fork cattlemen, who were just beginning to use the mountain meadows for summer cattle pasture. Old sheep trails criss-cross the mountains. The remains of one runs north into Rattlesnake Creek; parts of another are visible north of Kennedy Meadows.

The task of taking large bands of sheep into the rugged high country was by no means a small operation. Fallen timbers, rocky ledges, swift rivers, and sharp ridges above the timberline had to be dealt with before the sheep could reach the lush pastures.

The mountains had more than their share of predators, not only mountain lions and coyotes, but the small black bear and his big brother, the grizzly.

Another hazard was created by tribes of Owens Valley Indians who made annual sojourns to the Sierras. It didn't take many Indian braves to scare a couple of peaceful herders into turning over their meager supplies. Once, the herders made the mistake of offering the Indians whiskey in lieu of their few items of camp gear. A bad situation became impossible. If the sheepmen could not produce enough whiskey to satisfy the Indians, their sheep would be killed, often their prized sheep dogs, too. Sometimes the Indians would raid the herder's camp and take everything they could find. That meant a delay in the drive, while the terrified sheepmen

Grizzly bear killed on Olanche Peak by Pete Giraud in 1908.

made a long trip to get supplies, often as far as 200 miles round trip.

Barring attacks from wild animals and whiskey-crazy Indians, the herders still had a problem or two to deal with on the trails through the high country. When they came to a river crossing, they had to fall a large tree across the water, strip off all the branches and then carefully lead the sheep across. In 1916, Jules Conterno built a bridge of cable and split cedar at the western river crossing. It had two spans, supported in the middle by a large boulder in the river. It was unbelievably shaky, and it took a good deal of coaxing by the herders to get the lead ewe to venture out on the contraption, but once the first sheep braved the bridge the rest followed across meekly.

In the summer of 1889, a group of eight men from Bakersfield made a trip to Mt. Whitney. An account of the trip is contained in a book titled, *A Climb Through History*, by William Harland Boyd. The sheep became the subject of one of the earliest records of an ecological environmental impact report. It said:

"As the Mount Whitney climbers moved through the Sierra Nevada, they observed that the meadow grasses were being depleted. In Brown's Meadow, as elsewhere, there was evidence of over-grazing. Yearly, the crop of grasses is decreasing, and it is continually overstocked. Ere very long the meadows would become the deserts to all intents and purposes. Admittedly, it was trite to speak and rail about sheep, yet they were doing incalculable damage.

"By the treading of their countless feet, every shrub and tender tree was destroyed. They grazed clear into the ground, and in eating, they pulled very much of the forage up by the roots.

Wagon used to service A. Brown sheep camps at Manter and Big Meadow. Photo taken in 1914 shows the Manter cow camp in the left background.

"Their paths, trending longitudinally with the hills, formed water courses for winter storms which aggregated into torrents and cut deep gullies in every hillside. And then the herders, both willfully and carelessly, set fires in every direction.

"Willfully, to burn off brush and jungle that the next season's feed might be increased in area; carelessly, they built fires at the foot of trees and in all sorts of places to ward off wild animals.

"Sheep driving threatened to destroy the forest of the mighty Sierras, and by thus striking down that hand of nature which protected the snows and nurtured moist places, the smiling face of California valley lands would be changed to the dreary brown of a desert country. This should be prevented."

Some very harsh words about sheep grazing, but all the ranchers who were beginning to use the high country as summer pasture for their cattle felt that the sheepmen were ruining the range. True, the sheepmen tended to increase their flocks to the limits of nature, but the early cattlemen were also found guilty of overgrazing in many cases.

Another hazard for the sheepmen. Cattlemen.

Charlie Tibbetts, an old time resident of the Kern River Valley, loved to tell the story about the time he scared a herder out of the mountains.

It happened to be a year when the bears had a population explosion and Charles had killed three good-sized bears on the edge of Big Meadow within a week. He skinned them and then hauled them off into the trees and left them.

It was about a week later that a sheepherder came rushing into Charlie's camp, jabbering in French and broken English that somebody had killed three men.

Charlie realized that when a bear is skinned

out it very closely resembles a human carcass, and he also realized that the sheepherder probably didn't get close enough to the rotting bodies to see the difference, so he seized the opportunity to throw a good scare into the unwelcome intruder.

Straight-faced and serious, Charlie told the shaken sheepman that what he had seen were the remains of several sheepmen that he had ordered to leave the mountain meadows. They had refused, and Charlie admitted he'd done 'em in. Well, according to Charlie, that Frenchman made record time gathering up his sheep and leaving the mountains.

The creation of the Sequoia National Park in 1890, cut down on substantial numbers of grazing ranges available to sheepherders. The determined sheepmen didn't give up the lands without a fight. The Army was given custody of the Park in 1891 and several excerpts from official records indicate that they got little cooperation from the sheepmen.

"1892 — Entire season spent in trying to keep the sheep from the Park. Sheep most troublesome . . . the commanding officer was unable to ride out on an inspection tour as there was not a mouthful of feed left in the Park."

"1895 — Found that sheep had been moved into the Park when the troops left in the fall."

With the intensified patrol of the National Park lands, the numbers of sheep in the high country diminished each year, and the drought of 1897-99 cut down the numbers even further. There were signs posted on trees in the mountains that remained many years after the last band of sheep had come through. The signs were posted in English, Spanish, and French and read, NO SHEEP BEYOND THIS POINT.

The controversy over sheep using the National Park lands was only one facet of the sheepman's fight for survival. Range wars between the cattleman and the sheepman provided material for dozens of movies and books. The sheepman was either the mistreated underdog driven off into the sunset, or the odiferous hero who won the cattleman's daughter and the land-by-the-creek, after a bloody battle.

The animosity posed a major problem in many parts of the United States, but in the Kern River Valley there were many big ranchers, such as Andy Brown, who raised sheep until the grazing lands became too scarce, and then went into the

Alfred Giraud

cattle business. Brown's Meadow, described as "badly over-grazed" by the Mt. Whitney climbers in 1889, belonged to Andy Brown. It was one of two summer sheep camps owned by the A. Brown Company. Brown's Meadow, now known as Big Meadow, provided summer pasture for hundreds of cattle long after sheep were banned from the high country.

Two other valley ranchers, Art Alexander and Oscar Rudnick, ran both sheep and cattle in various parts of the county. They later established the thriving Onyx Ranch in the South Fork.

The partnership between Alexander, the Scotsman, and Rudnick, known to everyone as "the Old Man," had one cattle/sheep crisis that might have made a funny movie scene.

The two men purchased a new piece of ranch property, and Rudnick was dispatched to Nevada to buy cattle. For some reason, there were no desirable cattle available and Rudnick purchased a large band of sheep instead. He called Alexander and advised him that two carloads of stock would arrive the next day by railroad at Brown, a small town northwest of Ridgecrest.

Expecting Nevada cattle, Alexander arrived at Brown at the appointed time with his best bunch of cowboys. When the sheep were unloaded, nobody laughed.

Alexander's Scotch temper erupted, and the cowboys, who knew nothing about herding sheep, were so mad that they threatened to quit on the spot! When everyone finally calmed down, Alexander arranged to truck the sheep to the new ranch, where they were placed in a fenced pasture. No one repeated the conversation that took place between Rudnick and Alexander the next time they met, but I'll bet that the air rang with yowling and probably a good laugh or two.

Just as Rudnick and Alexander carved their names on the ranching history of Kern County, so did a great number of the sheepmen who came from Europe. Many of them worked for large ranches as herders and shearers until they accumulated enough money to buy sheep and start their own businesses. Their names are legend in the Bakersfield area. Their descendants have either continued in the sheep business, or become successful in other endeavors. They include such families as Ansolabehere, Etcheverry, Eyherabide, Mendiburru, Noriega, and Saldubehere.

There was another name, Alfred Giraud. He came to Bakersfield just as poor and just as hopeful as Faustino Noriega, and he was one of the last sheepmen to drive sheep over the "great circuit."

If I could have put an oil painting of the early sheepman in this book, it could not have been more true to life than the following memoir, beautifully written by Ken Wortley, publisher of the *Sierra Rainbow* (1954-58). Wortley is a man of many talents and experiences. He and his brother, Chet, worked as packers and guides in the Kern River country in the early years. They traveled with some of the great names of that era, such as Zane Grey. Wortley is a well-known

valley resident, now retired, and living in Black Gulch near Keyesville.

In the 1920's Ken worked for Alfred Giraud. He packed grub to the herders on the trail, took care of the horses and mules, and hunted strays. Giraud made an indelible impression on Ken and long after he'd left his employ, he visited the old sheepman to renew their friendship and interview him for the *Sierra Rainbow*.

"On a big ranch near Bishop stands a little one-room rock house. Its floor is earth. It is surrounded by clusters of wooden sheds and crude corrals. Inside at one end is a fireplace, a stack of sagebrush, an old air-bellows and an assortment of dutch ovens. The furniture is crude and antique. Along the walls are shelves well-stocked with groceries and jugs of fine French wine. Sacks of mutton jerky hang from rough-hewn rafters.

"A stranger would hardly surmise that the stocky old man with the long mustache, wearing thick-soled boots, worn dungarees, and faded denim shirt, who lives there was the owner of the big ranch and the herds of sheep and cattle grazing in its fields.

"These things the stranger may not guess, but of one thing he would soon be sure; that Alfred Giraud was a sheepman to the very core.

"Like most old sheepmen, Giraud either likes or dislikes a stranger almost instantly. If the latter is the case, he will let him do most of the talking and get rid of him as soon as possible, but if he likes him, he will invite him into his house, break out a bottle of wine, ask him to eat and entertain him with stories of his experiences.

"He may begin by telling of his first visit to Inyo County, that briefly would run something like this: 'Gee, but it was a glorious experience. It was wintertime, the wind she blow; Gollee! but it was cold. The stage from Mojave was too full of people. Because I am young and strong I ride on the seat with the driver. I have no coat, I have no bed, I have no money, I have no notheeng but the job of herding the sheep. Well I get to Bishop! Gol-lee! she was a beautiful hardship!'

"Alfred Giraud knows the Sierra and the desert country almost as well as he knows the inside of the little house. When he was a young man he herded sheep along the base of the Great Western Divide before the great upper basins of the Kern and the Kings River were set aside to include a portion of Sequoia National Park.

"At the edge of timberline near the head of Tyndall Creek in the shadow of towering Mt. Williamson, one of his camps remains intact and is sometimes used by pack parties who like to camp off the beaten trail.

"Giraud is possibly the last man to ever cross the Kern Kings divide with stock by way of Harrison Pass, the most rugged and dangerous in all the Sierras. Harrison Pass was abandoned years ago in favor of Junction Pass, which is now seldom used since the completion of Foresters Pass.

"Giraud remembers when the Kern River Canyon was set afire all the way from Kernville to the Kern Lakes each year to make forage for sheep and cattle.

"Like all real sheepmen, Giraud kept only the best stock. Besides a string of top saddle horses, he had two of the best saddle mules ever ridden.

"One time while we were camped at Indian Wells, an old prospector came into camp with three pack burros. One of them was a big blue Jack that caught Giraud's eye. Next to their dogs, there was nothing more prized by the sheepmen than an exceptional burro. I knew that Giruad was determined to have the burro and I was almost sure that the prospector would not part with him. After three days of dickering, however, the old man left, four hundred dollars richer in cash, with several gallons of wine, two goats, and a hangover that was a dilly, but minus his Jack.

"Pack burros were trained to follow the sheep. Once his flock began to move at daylight, especially in bad weather, a herder had no time to bother with packs. He was constantly on the move covering many miles over all sorts of terrain. When evening came, his burros must be with the sheep, their loads intact. All burros were not easily trained or able to stand up under heavy loads in rough mountain country, so for this reason a good burro was considered invaluable by the sheepmen.

"Burros, however, were secondary in importance to a sheepman's dogs. They were the lieutenants, the companions and the tireless, faithful helpers, without which it would have been impossible to herd sheep on the open range. A proven dog was one thing a sheepman would not part with. Through misfortune and difficulty, he might be forced to part with the horses, mules, burros and even his ranch, but he would keep his dogs.

"The best sheep dog was the Australian shepherd. Some of these animals seemed to possess almost human intelligence. It was uncanny the way they learned to obey the signals of the herders. Sometimes these signals were a mere gesture, but a well-trained dog knew instantly what he was supposed to do.

"As an example of how really good some of these marvelous dogs were, Giraud had one old Australian shepherd, named Bozo, that he had trained from a puppy. As a rule, when a dog became too old to be useful on the range, he would be left at one of the base camps with the tender, until he died of old age. When Old Bozo became too old to stand the regular duties, he refused to stay in camp unless chained day and night. He was determined to be with the sheep. Finally, Giraud let him go to keep up with the flocks as best he could. The faithful old dog took to following stragglers and many a sheep was saved by the dog. One day Bozo failed to make it back to camp and was never seen again.

"January that year at Indian Wells was extremely mild. From his base camp, Giraud ranged two bands of about 2,500 sheep each, along the barren mountains, between Indian Wells and Little Lake.

"Being an open winter, there was little feed in the lower hills bordering the desert, so the herders kept high up along the rim, at the head of the canyons for better grazing. This was rough and rugged country, even for sheep, and the herders and dogs worked almost constantly to keep their herds intact. Camps were made wherever there was room for a bedding ground. Sometimes these would be a little swale or a hidden valley often on the steep, sandy slopes of a canyon in a grove of yuccas, and once in a while on a point overlooking the valley.

"In good weather the herders camped in relative comfort, especially when the wind did not blow.

"Sometimes if their camps were too isolated for me to make a return trip to the base camp, after packing supplies, I would spend the night with the herders.

"On one of these occasions, we were camped high up on a point overlooking Indian Wells Valley. It was one of those warm, quiet nights that are so rare in January on the eastern slope of the Sierras. A little below camp, 3,000 sheep

A band of sheep travel through the South Fork Valley.

were bedded down for the night. The musical tinkle of the bells of the leaders and the bleat of restless sheep were the only sounds in the air.

"Somewhere, far down in the valley, the lights of a little town blinked in the night. It was Saturday and a dance was probably in progress. I knew that the young herders who sat beside me longed to be down there where there was gaiety and laughter, but I also learned that the lonely life of a sheepherder and the sacrifice of the pleasures of youth was the price these lads from the Pyrenees were willing to pay to satisfy their ambitions. His heart was set on someday becoming a big sheepman like his employer. His education must come from books read by the light of a campfire and his wisdom absorbed from the voices of solitude. No matter where his lonely bed in the future might be, in the shadow of a snow-clad mountain, amid rushing streams and whispering pines or the meager shelter of a greasewood fire on a cold and windswept flat, his dreams would always be of the success of tomorrow. This was a sheepman's philosophy.

"We sat there on the mountain side and talked late into the night; far too late, for the sheep would be moving at daylight and another hard day lay ahead for the young herder.

"Finally the lights down below went out one by one. The glow of a rising moon began to show in the east beyond the hump of Mt. Argus; a coyote yelped on a distant ridge, and the dogs were streaks in the night.

"Life at the base camp of the sheepmen was entirely different from that of the herders. Here was comfort and the luxury of varied companionship.

"There was always plenty to eat and red wine to wash it down. The sheepmen were the finest camp cooks in the world and as bakers of sourdough bread, were unequaled masters.

"It seems strange that out of a band of 2,000 sheep, there were always a few that a good sheepman could distinguish from the rest. Once in a while one of these would be singled out as a leader when a band was formed.

"One day an old ewe that Giraud intended to retain as a leader turned up missing, and he

Alfred Giraud 1900.

asked me to saddle up and see if I could pick up her track before the coyotes got her.

"I hunted two days, picking up several strays including a ewe and a lamb that two coyotes had chased up into a pile of rocks, but never found the sheep I was looking for. Three years later, Giraud found her at Monache Meadow in the Sierras, proving that all stray sheep do not fall prey to predators.

"The weather remained beautiful right up to the middle of February, with a twang of Indian Summer still in the air. Then came the end of as beautiful a winter day as ever smiled upon the desert hills of Indian Wells Valley. The evening sky was clear and bright and the atmosphere enhanced with unnatural softness.

"There were no radio reports in those days to warn of a sudden change in the weather, but the sheepmen were good at predicting a coming storm. Alfred Giraud was no exception as a weather prophet. Something told him that his herders were going to need help before morning. After supper he saddled up a mule, packed another and left for the sheep with his dogs.

"I was awakened at dawn by the roar of the wind. Beyond the portal of the dugout where my bed was made, greasewood with writhing shapes, were dancing crazily in a blur of drifting snow. Winter had arrived suddenly during the night.

"Borne on the wings of an arctic wind, the storm had swept down from the north through the high Sierra passes in a matter of a few hours. By daylight Indian Wells Valley was in the grip of the worst blizzard ever on record.

"In the teeth of this blizzard, somewhere up on the divide between Sand and Noname Canyon, Giraud and his four herders with their dogs were fighting to hold five thousand sheep from drifting with the wind. There would be little protection on the barren mountainside against the force of the storm and no rest for men or dogs if the sheep were to be kept intact. Once they began to separate they would scatter in every direction. To prevent this would test the mettle of a born sheepman. It was an emergency for which Alfred Giraud and his boys from the Alps had been trained from childhood to meet.

"For three days and three nights the blizzard howled without let-up. The dawn of the fourth day broke clear and cold, with an 18-inch blanket of snow covering the Valley. The slope of the Sierras was a mass of white, and beyond the Matarangos to the northeast, Telescope Peak in the Panamints resembled a great iceberg glistening in the distance.

"During the storm, the grizzled camp tender and myself remained in the dugout in comparative comfort. We were not sheepmen and there was nothing we could do to help Giraud and his herders. Now that the storm was over, there was plenty to do. If the sheep had been saved and were together, they must be fed and soon.

"I helped the tender hitch up his team and load some hay — then I saddled up and started out with a pack mule loaded with supplies, to find Giraud.

"About two miles from camp, I found a band of seven sheep huddled together on a knoll, blown partly clear of snow, but they were not carrying Giraud's brand. I learned later that they were part of a band of two thousand sheep that had been lost near Little Lake the first night of the storm. The head herder of this band had become sick, another herder had gone to Little Lake for help and a third, a Mexican, could not handle the dogs. The whole band had scattered across the desert to starve.

"I found Giraud with his two bands almost intact in the shelter of the mouth of Noname Canyon. He had succeeded in working the sheep down off the ridge to the spot and man-

A herder's lonely life on the Mojave Desert taken at 6 a.m.

aged to hold the herds together.

"The sheep were fed hay at this place until the snow melted from the valley floor and then Giraud moved them in the shelter of the lava formations bordering the desert south of Little Lake where it was warm, and the brush was green.

"Heavy rains drenched the Valley in March and by the first of April the desert was a sea of flowers. A month later the filiree was a foot high and the sheep round and fat.

"It was one of those springs for which a stockman hopes and dreams, but seldom sees in a lifetime on the open range.

"Things looked good to Alfred Giraud. He had saved his sheep from the blizzard where other sheepmen failed. The market was tops because of heavy losses by others due to the storm.

"About this time, when things looked the most rosy, Giraud made a fateful decision. He accepted a proposition and bought a summer range between the Argus and Coso Mountains from a Lone Pine cowman. This range included a large portion of land now within the U.S. Naval Ordinance Test Station proving grounds in the mountains northeast of China Lake and the present city of Ridgecrest.

"This transaction which was apparently agreeably completed, was the beginning of a chain of reverses for Giraud which might have driven a weaker man to murder or suicide.

"The first low blow was struck shortly after Giraud had spent several thousand dollars building watering troughs and had moved his sheep on his new range. This range included a mining claim at the mouth of Mountain Spring Canyon where he had established a permanent base camp.

"We were eating breakfast here under the cottonwoods one morning watching a covey of quail coming in to water, when one of the herders barged into camp. He was so excited he could hardly talk. I could not understand what he finally told Giraud because he spoke in French, but whatever it was, I knew it wasn't good.

"I didn't wait to ask questions, but got the Model T cranked up and the three of us climbed in and we started up the canyon. I was curious all the way up the fifteen miles of winding mountain road to know what the trouble was, but refrained from asking questions since Giraud offered no explanation.

"We reached the summit and drove across a mesa toward a group of low hills. In a few mi-

53

Giraud and his dogs, 1910

nutes, I did not need to be told what the trouble was. The hillside was covered with dead sheep. Someone had sprayed the brush with cyanide. Out of five thousand sheep, half were dead and the other half either sick or ready to die.

"I think counting those dead sheep and trying to save the others were the worst hours of Alfred Giraud's life. He had paid fifteen thousand dollars for the range and it had taken him twenty years to build up his herd. He had accomplished an almost impossible task in saving these sheep when disaster threatened only to lose them through treachery.

"The loss of his sheep and the threat of other reverses was too much for Giraud. He decided to give up his range, forfeit his losses, and return to his ranch at Bishop.

"I had made other arrangements, but under the circumstances agreed to take Giraud's stock north for him. After arriving at the Bishop ranch, I waited two weeks for the sheep that had survived the poisoning to arrive.

"In those days there were no trucks to transport sheep and cattle like there are today. Flocks of sheep from Bakersfield were still trailed over the old immigrant road to Mono County as late as the early thirties.

"With his sheep in his home pastures, Giraud was soon happy and optimisic again. After all, he still had his ranch and enough sheep left for a new start. With a little luck, in a few years, his herds would again roam the open range. His ranch was not clear, but he had ninety-thousand dollars in the bank with which to pay off the mortgage any time he wished.

"The day came when I was ready to leave. Giraud drove me down to catch the morning bus south.

"Driving down the main street of Bishop, we noticed a large group of people milling about in front of the Waterson Brothers Bank where Giraud did business. The crowd seemed excited so we parked the car across the street and walked over to see what the trouble was.

"We knew what had happened even before we noticed the sign posted in the glass window of the bank's front door which read: 'Owing to circumstances beyond our control, this bank has been forced to close': the bank had failed.

"Two years later while driving through the South Fork Valley of the Kern near Onyx, I met a band of about three hundred sheep in the road. The herder was Alfred Giraud and with him were the same dogs that had helped save the sheep during the blizzard at Noname Canyon. Following behind was the big blue jack with a pack on his back that Giraud obtained from the old prospector at Indian Wells.

"This was all that Giraud had managed to salvage, but it proved in time to be sufficient to make a dream come ture — the dreams of a lad herding sheep on the wild slopes of the French Alps a half century earlier.

"Today, on his ranch in Bishop, surrounded by the peaks of the Sierras, in a setting closely akin to the land of his early childhood across the sea, Alfred lives in the twilight of that dream.

"As he sits before the glowing embers of his fireplace in his little rock house on cold winter nights, the great barren ridges, the blinding blizzards, the seas of desert flowers and a multitude of experiences connected with the life of a sheepman, again become realities.

"So ends the saga of a sheepman, but there remains an inspiring picture that will always be indelibly implanted in my memory — the picture of Alfred Giraud, standing hatless, facing the wind in the ruddy glow of the sunset, tending his sheep on a wild mountain ridge, high above Indian Wells Valley."

The men like Giraud and Noriega grew old, their memories and their remarkable heritage passed on through the years to sons and grandsons who would continue to follow in the proud, solitary footsteps of their forefathers.

In 1934, the Taylor Grazing Act ended the unlimited use of open range to sheep and cattle. Ranchers were required to have a permit to graze herds on federal lands such as the Sequoia National Park. Those permits carefully limited the number of animals per acre so that there would be no overgrazing.

While the sheep owners searched for new ranges, land became big business in the San Joaquin Valley. Cattle and agricultural ventures boomed.

The Kern County Land Company, established in 1890, was for years one of the nation's leading suppliers of meat and wool. In the 1930's they sold all their sheep interests to Oscar Rudnick and Gregorio Mendiburru. They later sold all their land and other diversified interests to Tenneco.

The sheep owners closed ranks and organized their operations. They joined the Western Range Association, which offered a variety of services including hiring herders from the old country.

For a fee, which guaranteed the herder a round-trip fare and a three-year contract, the WRA handled all the arrangements for the sheep owner. Some herders arrived with a tag on their coats which read, "Ship to the Noriega Hotel, Bakersfield." Like Faustino Noriega, they spoke little English — but unlike Noriega, they were offered shelter and sponsorship.

A few stayed only long enough to fulfill their contract, then returned to their native home with savings of more then $8,000. Some received a "green card" from their employer which allowed them to stay in the country indefinitely, whether they continued to work as herders or not. However, most of them continued doing the work they were trained for and stayed with the sheep.

There were many who worked on the large ranches, learning, and saving their money, until they were eventually able to buy a flock of their own. These devoted sheepmen and their families contributed their unique knowledge toward building Kern County into a top-ranking region of the sheep industry.

The days of the "great circuit" were over, and they had to find grazing lands other than the high country meadows, or provide for pasture and ranch facilities. As a result, smaller ranches were established, and herds were reduced to a more manageable size.

As land values increased and the population in all areas of the San Joaquin Valley continued to grow, the familiar sheep driveways were closed. Traffic made it impractical to move the sheep along old routes such as Highway 395 into the desert. It was cheaper to truck the sheep to graz-

Old photo of five thousand sheep in Monache Meadows, 1900.

ing lands in less populated places such as Mono County, or even into other states where there was still open range available. The sheepmen took advantage of range land wherever they could find it, and then trucked the sheep back to home ranches in Kern County for lambing and shearing.

Today, there are very few large, privately owned sheep ranches in Kern County. The same families are active sheep owners, but they move the bands out of county and out of state during the late spring, summer, and early fall months to graze. Usually in October, the sheep are trucked back into Kern County where many sheepmen contract with farmers to rent their land so that the sheep can feed from field to field on the alfalfa stubble.

The greatest change in the industry came with the promotion of lamb sales for meat consumption. Profit from wool sales was low, and with the introduction of spring lamb (six months) for the table, public demand for lamb provided the best cash crop for the sheep owner.

The 1976 census, taken in January, recorded 153,000 head of sheep quartered here, making Kern County No. 1 in sheep production in the state. Sheep and lamb sales were $8.2 million dollars, an average of $54.45 per hundred weight. According to the Kern County Agriculture Department, the major breeds being raised are Suffolk, Hampshire, and Crossbreeds.

Wool production in 1976 totaled 1,637,000 pounds, with a unit value of 64.2 cents per pound, valued at $1,051,000 dollars. The average

55

shearing costs run about 75 cents per head — a far cry from the five cents a fleece Bat Albitre earned hand-shearing in Leopold Vignave's sheds at Granite Station.

There are very few heroic stories about sheepherders among the tales of the great western adventure. We built legends around the antics of cattle barons, cowboys, lawmen, and even outlaws, but the sheepherder remains an enigma. Frontiersmen, in every sense of the word, these fiercely independent, rugged men pioneered one of Kern County's major industries.

The Basque sheepherder probably knew more about the Sierra Nevada high country than most ecologists. They traveled it in every season, knew every precarious ridge and water crossing, every sign the land gave, and certainly every singular beauty of each meadow and wandering trail. What did they think about while they walked the "great circuit?" What did they learn from the land on the Kern Plateau and the Mojave Desert?

I guess the best way to sum up the sheepherder's philosophy and his way of life is to use the words of one of their own, Alfred Giraud. "Goll-lee, she was a beautiful hardship!!"

Alfred Giraud

IV
Bodfish

THE LITTLE TOWN of Bodfish lay in the foothills below what was known in the early days as Hot Springs Hill. It was first called Bodfish in 1892, when a post office was established there. The name was chosen from nearby Bodfish Creek.

In the late 1850's George H. Bodfish came to the Kern River Mines and set up a gold stamp mill below Keyesville. After the mill was destroyed in the 1861-62 flood, he left the valley and went up to the Piutes where he operated a store in the mining camp of Claraville. He eventually settled in a wooded canyon that now carries his name.

There is some speculation that a mining discovery in 1888 on Bodfish Creek may have brought George Bodfish back into the Kern

Kernville Caliente stage, 1902 at the "Vaughn" Post Office.

River area, but his name doesn't appear in any official records. The mining activity on Bodfish Creek was mentioned in the State Mineralogist's report and stated only that a claim had been registered by Wales L. Palmer and two steam arrastras were under construction.

By 1896, the claim had been named the Glen Olive Mines. There were seven claims, still under the ownership of Palmer who was listed as a resident of San Francisco. That year there had been three tunnels developed on the vein at 100 feet, 150 feet, and 200 feet. The vein was six to nine inches wide and the quartz contained a heavy percentage of sulphurets. Where there were sulphurets present the gold particles were coated with sulphur compounds and would not amalgamate with mercury. A process called cyanidation was used, in which the gold was dissolved in weak solution of sodium cyanide and then passed through zinc shavings, where the gold adhered to the zinc.

By 1913, the Glen Olive Mines were the largest producer in the Pioneer Mining District, which lay between Clear Creek and Erskine Creek, on 120 acres of land in the Sequoia Forest Reserve. The owner in that year was A. W. Stetson of San Francisco, and the superintendent was F. A. Braden. There were two veins about 200 feet apart — named the Russian Bear and the Bulgarian Troubles! The average width of the vein was three feet. The ore was free milling, and produced about $25 gold per ton on the plates. The pay shoot was 200 feet long, and the workings consisted of two tunnels on the vein about 200 feet apart and 700 feet long. Mine equipment included ore cars, an 800-foot automatic tramway, shops, assay office, and dwellings. There was a Hendy mill with 1,000-pound stamps, driven by a gasoline powered engine.

Bodfish School, 1918 — Miss Bessie Nelson, teacher.

(Gas was 12 cents a gallon then!) Water for the mill was obtained from nearby springs, and the tailings were impounded in a gulch. Total production since discovery was $500,000.

That was the last entry for the claims; the Glen Olive Mines were closed in May of 1914. The reason listed was general financial conditions, and due to an extensive amount of work that

The Fussell family with some of their pets, 1914. Ruby, with kitten, Ruth with a lamb, Charlie with burro, Fred with kid.

needed to be done on the vein. The site of the Glen Olive Mines is still visible in 1979, and the stamp mill is of exceptional historical value since it is still in fair condition.

The first Bodfish post office was in the home of Edward Vaughn, who also served as postmaster. The Vaughn homestead was located several hundred yards south of the present junction of the Borel overhead flume and Old Highway 178. The remains of two black oak trees that once shaded the Vaughn home are still visible on the west side of the road.

The post office continued to operate officially under the name of Bodfish until 1895, when it was closed. It was re-opened in 1897, but the township was now called Vaughn. Edward Vaughn resumed his duties as postmaster and served until 1904.

The history of Bodfish is closely woven around the members of several families — the Vaughns, the Rhodehamels, and the Fussells. Early pioneer Edward Vaughn and his wife, May, were among the first residents. Their daughter, Grace, was married to Arthur Rhohamel in 1895, and they took up residence in Bodfish.

The Bodfish school starts the day with prayer. Teacher, Miss Bessie Nelson, year 1918.

The Rhodehamels had two children, Daisy and Wesley. When they were old enough to start school, the children rode two-and-a-half miles on their burros to attend classes at the Palmer School. In 1905, the Palmer School District was dissolved, and the Isabella School District and the Vaughn School District were established. A new schoolhouse was built in Old Isabella and another in Bodfish.

Daisy remembers her first teacher in the new Vaughn school was Miss Leo Herzinger. All the children were permitted to call the schoolmarm "Miss Leo," since the last name seemed to be a tongue-twister for the students.

The Vaughn School District was officially formed on April 3, 1905, and John Neill served as district clerk from 1905 to 1912. The district began with an average daily attendance of ten pupils.

Miss Leo Herzinger stayed with the school for its first five years. In 1910, in a memo to the school board she noted, "The only thing we need is a nine months term, instead of an eight months term. The children are good and studious but a trifle slow."

Jim and Leo Polkinghorne on their wedding day.

Bodfish Post Office, 1914. Truthful Brown on the porch.

The Vaughn School District was always small; the average daily attendance never exceeded 22 pupils, but the area increased in 1920 when the Havilah School District was annexed. Mrs. Leanah Schanz had the longest term of any Vaughn teacher—1930 to 1942. The little school district continued to serve Bodfish and Havilah children until January 23, 1950, when the Vaughn School was annexed to the Kernville Union School District.

In 1914, Daisy Rhodehamel married Jack Old-field, who was working for the Forest Service out of the Isabella station. Except for the time spent at various lookout stations during fire season, the Oldfields lived in Bodfish. In 1978, Daisy was still living in her comfortable home on land that was part of the original Vaughn homestead.

May Vaughn retired from her duties at the post office in 1906-07 and Charles Harding became postmaster. He served only for one year, but during that year the decision was made to re-name the post office — Bodfish. The name continues to draw amused looks from visitors and the routine question, "What kind of a fish is a

Store, boarding house and post office — Bodfish 1911.

Bodfish?" Only the oldtimers remember the pioneer for whom the town was named.

One of the most colorful members of the Bodfish community was E. G. "Truthful" Brown. Brown was postmaster from 1907 until 1929. His first name remained a mystery since he was known to everyone as Truthful Brown, a nickname he earned because of his talents as a storyteller. He vied for storytelling honors with other Hot Springs Valley neighbors such as Bill Murray and George King, both from Old Isabella.

Daisy Oldfield recalled several of his wild stories. One of them, in particular, should have won him a tall tales award. It seems the main topic at one story-telling session was the winding, crooked canyon road down to Hobo Hot Springs. According to Truthful Brown, that road was so crooked that during the trip, when he was hauling hay down the canyon, he kept hearing these strange noises behind him. He tried to look back each time he heard the noise, but most of his attention had to be directed at keeping his team on that crooked road. Finally, on one of the sharpest curves he happened to look back just in time to see what the noise was. The lead horses were eating the hay from the back of the loaded wagon on every curve. Now that's a crooked road!

In those days there was only a post office in Bodfish. Then in 1911 Mr. and Mrs. Fleming opened the boarding house and store adjoining the post office.

In 1915, the tempo of life in Bodfish picked up a bit. The county engineering department staked out a new roadway on the west side of the Kern Canyon, south of Bodfish. It was to replace the old stage road on the opposite side.

A miner ready to leave Culbertson Store in Bodfish.

The resident engineer was a young fellow named Chet Young. Chet came up to Bodfish from Stockton to direct the highway project, and moved into a little cabin just north of the post office. He boarded with Louie and May Coppel, along with Truthful Brown and the Ross brothers. May Coppel's home-cooked meals were still fond memories for Chet after fifty years. He says he can still taste the fresh vegetables from May's garden and the trout and game Louie provided for the table — all prepared in grand style.

The road project began in the spring of 1915 and was scheduled to take three or four months. Chet had as many as 140 men on the crew when the bad weather set in. Rain, rain and more rain. The hillsides were too slippery to work on and the men were forced to sit around in their tents as long as forty days at a time. The construction camp was located on the flat at the foot of Hot Springs Hill. The delays more than doubled construction time, and it was nine months before the job was finished.

Chet described the road building as follows: Using horse-drawn plows and makeshift equipment, the crews tackled some really rough terrain. First, a sidehill plow was pulled across the slope by a team of two or three horses, one in

Mr. and Mrs. Fleming, 1903.

Bodfish Water Company

Neighbors stop for a visit as they meet on the hill above Bodfish.

front of the other, to remove part of the hillside. Second, they used a specially built V-plow with a long wing-shaped blade on one side, loaded with rocks in the center to make the blade cut deep. When the V-plow had cut out a wide enough path, the contractors were able to bring in scrapers pulled by four-horse teams.

All the dirt removed from the road-bed was dumped over the side of the canyon. Highway engineering was much simpler in those days, no "environmental impact" rules. Dumping the dirt into the canyon also eliminated long hauls. Some of the contractors that were hired to work on the dirt removal project included Bledsow & Castro and John Hooper. Chet said he'd never seen any man do so much work with so little help and equipment as John Hooper. He said that Hooper worked the same way at everything he tackled, whether it was a road, building an adobe house, or setting up a gold stamp mill.

Besides the bad weather, Chet had to put up with mysterious visitors that kept moving the road stakes in the middle of the night. The county surveyor had to come from Bakersfield on three different occasions to reset the boundaries. Chet said the road was probably two or three feet off by the time it was completed. Though it wasn't much of a road, it was certainly a lot better to travel than the stage route on the other side of the canyon.

Since the construction on the road stretched into the winter months, Chet welcomed the chance to get away from the pleasures of his job by riding horseback down the canyon to Democrat Hot Springs. It was a twelve mile trip, but well worth the long ride to join Jim and Leo (Herzinger) Polkinghorn for good food and pleasant company in the resort dining room.

Another pioneer family took up residence in Bodfish in 1909. Herman Fussell and his wife, and their four children, Charley, Fred, Ruth, and Ruby, added to the family atmosphere of the township. The children were a welcome addition to the Vaughn School, and the family joined the Vaughns and the Rhodehamels in the little community. With the exception of these families, the population was mostly single miners like the Ross brothers.

62

L to R, Ben Werth, Ruth Fussell Werth, Ruby Fussell and unidentified friend.

As the Fussell boys grew older, they worked in the gold mines with their father. For many years they worked at the Mammoth Mill on the Kern River, traveling to and from work over the old swinging bridge that crossed the Kern River between Bodfish and the mill. They also worked at the Keyes Mine for a time, and lived in Keyesville.

Ruth Fussell married Ben Werth in 1922, when he was employed at the Borel power plant as an operator. Ben worked for Southern California Edison Company for 35 years, mostly in the Kern River Valley. For the last fifteen years of his career, he was divisional superintendent at the KR-1 plant.

Among the families to settle near Bodfish in the 1900's were the Otto Liebels, who lived several miles up Erskine Creek; the Albert Bradens, and the Fred Helmans, who lived in Bodfish Canyon.

In 1921, Jack and Ida Harrington purchased the Helman homestead. They had three children — Vern, Oliver, and Elsie. Vern and Oliver attended the Vaughn School, but Elsie was already out of school when they came to Bodfish Canyon. She later married Wes Rhodehamel and

they moved to Havilah, where Wes went to work for the Forest Service. After a tour of duty with the Forest Service, Wes was employed by the Edison Company and worked for them for 36 years.

Oliver Harrington homesteaded just above the family ranch in Bodfish Canyon. His land is now a popular subdivision known as Canyon Meadows. Oliver was killed in Manila during World War II.

Vern Harrington ran cattle in the forest above Bodfish Canyon. When the original Helman home burned down, Vern built another house on the Harrington Ranch. In 1978, the house was occupied by the Murtin E. Kearns family. The rest of the Helman-Harrington lands are now the Canyon Heights subdivision.

One of those best remembered by Bodfish residents is Verna Jensen. Verna and her son, Bruce, came to Bodfish in 1925 to visit her oldest son, Clayton. Verna and Bruce rode up the rugged canyon road on Phil Hand's mail stage. It was only the second day that the lower section of the road, from KR-1 to Democrat Hot Springs, had been opened. The trip from Bakersfield to Bodfish took three hours.

Jack and Daisy Oldfield, and daughter Florence.

Shortly after Verna arrived in Bodfish, the Culbertson store was put up for sale. Verna decided it was a golden opportunity to go into business for herself, so she bought it. The store and hand-pump filling station was located at the junction of the Havilah-Caliente Road and the Kern Canyon Road. The post office was also located in the store, with Truthful Brown as postmaster.

Through the store, Verna made countless friends and became a well-loved member of the community. In 1930, she took over the duties of postmistress when Truthful Brown retired. She held the office until 1955.

From 1955 until 1958, Mernie Silicz Mulkey was acting postmistress. Elizabeth Norris took over in 1958 and served for the next nineteen years. She moved with the growing number of Bodfish customers to the new brick post office building at the junction of the Bodfish-Caliente Road and Highway 178. Mrs. Norris was assisted in her duties by Charlotte French, who served from 1968 until both women retired in 1977. In 1978, Gary Kimball became the first man to hold the head postal job in Bodfish since the days of Truthful Brown.

By 1979, not much remained of Bodfish as it had been in the early days. Several of the old family names, such as Fussell, were used as street names in the new subdivisions, but the rest of the traditions were memories. The hillsides were now dotted with mobile homes, and new pads for more such modern living accommodations were being bulldozed each day.

The most familiar glimpse of the past is through the eyes of Daisy Oldfield and her sister-in-law, Elsie Rhodehamel, who still live in their homes on the old Vaughn homestead. These lovely ladies visit with their oldtime friends and spend many happy hours reminiscing about Bodfish in the good, old days.

V

Miracle Hot Springs

IN THE LATE 1870's this picturesque riverside camp was known as Compressor Hot Springs or Clear Creek Hot Springs. Situated about seven miles downstream from Isabella township on the Kern River, the site lay close to the lower end of Clear Creek, a waterway that originated on the Piutes.

Both names came about as the result of the efforts of an enterprising fellow, E. B. Sherman, who built a ditch to bring water from the Kern River to power a 54-inch water turbine.

The turbine had been shipped by rail to Caliente, then by freight team over the rugged roads of Walker Basin to the gold rush mining town of Havilah. Just north of Havilah, Sherman had cleared a roadway so that the turbine could be hauled down to the Clear Creek site.

The power generated by Sherman's turbine ran an air compressor, which boosted air through an eight inch pipe laid five miles up the mountainside to Havilah. It supplied air to the miners working in underground shafts, and operated the first air-powered drills used in California.

Unfortunately, the ingenious operation didn't last long. In 1879, a disgruntled miner who had been fired from a mill job in Havilah decided to get even by setting fire to five stamp mills. He then proceeded down Clear Creek and burned down Sherman's power plant.

The miner was caught and sentenced to ten years in prison for attempting to destroy the town of Havilah, but the compressor plant that had furnished air to the mountain mines was never restored to service.

In 1901, while the Borel power plant was under construction about a mile north of Compressor Hot Springs, some of the workers went on strike and moved out of company quarters. They set up camp near the springs, and per-suaded the local constable, Fred McCracken, to act as their go-between in dealing with the contractors. While the negotiations went on, the striking workers managed to raise the dander of nearby cattle ranchers by helping themselves to a cow or two. The irate cattlemen complained to the constable, who was reported to have growled, "Ah, they're just a bunch of hobos."

From that day on, the riverside camp was called Hobo Hot Springs. To accommodate miners and contruction crews working at Borel, two bathhouses were built near the river. They were cement tubs sunk into the hillside using the hot springs water supplied by gravity flow.

The camp was a popular gathering place and a favorite fishing spot, made even more accessible to visitors when the road between Bodfish and Democrat was completed in 1905-6.

Bath house at Hobo, 1903.

The installation of several hydroelectric plants on the Kern River made the need for a road from Bakersfield to the Kern River Valley a number one priority. However, it was not until the fall of 1926 that the first traffic traveled from Isabella to Bakersifield on the winding Kern Canyon Road.

A new era in Hobo Hot Springs history began in 1927. John L. Hooper and his son, Marion, obtained a permit from the Forest Service to lease the lands at Hobo Hot Springs to build a small hotel. The remains of Sherman's old power plant were still there, and the Hoopers were issued an additional permit to reconstruct the plant.

The Hooper clan was well-known among the pioneer families in the Kern River Valley. John was truly a "jack-of-all-trades" and a master of many. He was considered a quiet man, but he enjoyed a good joke and lasting friendships with miners and businessmen alike. His good humor and personal sense of fair play endeared him to all.

John Logan Hooper was born in Marion, Illinois on February 19, 1870, to Richard and Jane Cox Hooper. The family left Illinois and came west to settle in Kernville in the summer of 1874.

John's father was a cabinet and coffin maker, and proprietor of a small grocery store. The tools of his father's building trade must have fascinated young John, because he showed a keen interest in construction at a very early age.

When he was four, he began the ambitious job of building a dam across the Kern River. His mother interfered with the project and hauled him in to supper, but it was the beginning of a lifetime of "projects."

In those days, grade school education required ten years instead of the present eight years. John graduated from the Kernville school, but his plans for further formal education were cut short by the death of his father.

John was fifteen years old at the time of his father's death. He and his older brother, Tom, took over the operation of the grocery store, and John continued his education by taking correspondence courses in a number of technical subjects. Among the books he purchased was a five-volume set, "The Cyclopedia of Applied Electricity," published in 1905.

The brothers operated the store together for a year or so, then Tom took half the stock, moved his family over the mountains to the little town of Woody, and opened a store there.

By the age of nineteen, John was a seasoned store-keeper, but he was restless. He sold the store to a traveling salesman named Louder and directed his energies toward a number of mining operations.

Hoopers' adobe house — Old Isabella.

In 1893, he built a quartz mill on Greenhorn Mountain. His interest in mining and milling was stimulated by his technical studies and his construction know-how. The mining business remained a foremost challenge throughout his life.

In 1894, at the age of 24, John met and married Gwenevere Wyatt, a young schoolteacher from Kernville. They had three sons, Wyatt, Marion, and Jack.

In 1895, John formed a brief partnership with Fred Tibbetts. The two men bought the Mammoth Mine in Keyesville and began construction of a water-powered quartz mill to process the ore from the mine. The mill site was located on the banks of the Kern River, about one mile north of Old Isabella. By the time they had finished the mill, the mysterious Mammoth was having another of its periodic production lows, so Hooper and Tibbetts sold the mine and opened the mill for custom work (milling ore for other miners).

Business was slow, and there was only enough mill work for one man, so John took Gwenevere

John Hooper

Hooper's adobe blacksmith shop — Old Isabella.

and their baby son, Wyatt, and moved to Garlock, California, to the site of the famed Yellow Astor Mine. It was a rich mine, but ore had to be shipped to a mill six miles away. Hooper wanted to build a mill in a draw close to the mine, but his plans backfired when a timbering accident nearly cost him his life.

John returned to Hot Springs Valley with his family in 1897. He and his younger brother, Albert, bought out Fred Tibbetts' interest in the Kern River mill, and operated it successfully for the next seven years.

It was during these years in custom milling that John earned the nickname, "Honest John." Customers werre not allowed to leave the mill while their ore was being run. Hooper insisted that they stay and watch every operation, including the clean-up of plates and the melting down processes, so that there would be no question of "high-grading." The nickname remained with him the rest of his days, a badge of honor which he cherished.

In 1904, John and Albert sold the mill and the water rights to the Kern River Light and Power Company, the forerunner of the Southern California Edison Company, for the further construction of the hydroelectric system on the Kern River.

In 1905, John purchased land from Steven Barton in Isabella near the South Fork bridge. He built a two-story adobe house for his family and an adobe blacksmith shop just across the road. With his usual ingenuity, he provided power for both the house and the shop by installing a power windmill. The windmill provided power for a band-saw, turning lathe, and drill press. The shop did a lot of business during the construction of the Kern River Power plant.

1905 was a busy year. John and Albert built a new schoolhouse at Isabella, and the old adobe dance hall. No one in the district knew as much about building with adobe as Hooper. Some of his adobe buildings are still standing in 1979.

Another venture in 1905 was a bottling works

"Honest John" Hooper.

Old adobe house built by John Hooper in 1912. Still in use on the Hanning Ranch in 1979.

in Isabella, which continued to operate for several years. John and Albert also found time to work a ranch on lands that extended for a mile east of Old Isabella.

Work in the blacksmith shop slowed down in 1908 due to the completion of the major part of the Borel power plant. John left Albert in charge and moved his family to National City. There he built a cyanide plant to work a quantity of ore tailings which had been left behind by an off-shore Mexican mining venture.

John remained in National City until 1912, when he returned to the South Fork Valley at the request of John Cross. Cross wanted Hooper to build a small house for him and put in a well and a windmill. The Cross homestead is now part of the Weaver Hand ranch in Kelso Valley.

While working at the Cross homestead, John and Albert decided to take advantage of all the lands opening up to the west of town, and they took up homesteads of their own. By the fall of 1912, John had finished the work on the Cross ranch and completed an adobe house on his own land. Gwenevere and the children returned to their new home before winter began.

In 1913, the brothers contracted to build a new schoolhouse at Weldon to replace the one that had burned down. That same year they sold their Isabella property to Everett True and built a stamp mill at the Keyes Mine for the new owners from National City. John operated the mill for the National City group for the next eight years, on a part-time basis. During the last year, he acted as mine superintendent, and Gwenevere ran a boardinghouse for the miners.

In 1915, Hooper and Jeff Gillam contracted to build two miles of road on the south side of Bodfish Hill, a project which really tested their endurance.

John, then into his '50s, was always busy with small construction jobs, erecting windmills,

Hobo Hot Springs Hotel.

water tanks, wells and pumping plants in all parts of the Kern River Valley. He was 57 years old when he and his son, Marion, decided to build the Hobo Hot Springs hotel.

Marion, born in 1898, was the only surviving son. Wyatt died at age four and Jack died when he was thirty. Marion had attended elementary schools in Kernville and National City, and attended high school in Bakersfield. He worked with John and Albert in mining and construction, at the bottle works in Isabella, and had a hand in most of the various Hooper projects during the years. He also ran a trucking line out of the South Fork Valley, hauling cattle and sheep and supplies. He proudly recalls that he drove the first truckload of cattle over the new Kern Canyon Road when it opened in the fall of 1926. He says, with Hooper humor, "I'll let someone else drive the last load down!"

It was Marion who first learned that the Forest Service was going to lease lands along the new road for public use. He and John recognized the potential of the Hobo Hot Springs area and in 1927 they signed a long-term lease with the government to build a hotel just west of Hobo Campgrounds. The remains of Sherman's old compressor plant were still visible, and the Hoopers received permission to rebuild the power plant.

The Hobo Hot Springs Resort was a fine example of John Hooper's talents in construction. By 1928, the main hotel building had been completed on the river side of the road and a garage built on the opposite side of the Kern Canyon Road.

The original hotel building had three stories — the lower floor or basement had the hot baths and two apartments; the ground floor had a cafe, a small store and the post office annex; the third floor had four hotel rooms.

In the next two years, the Hoopers added four more rooms above the cafe for visitors. In addition to the hotel accommodations, there were eighteen cottages and a trailer park with twenty spaces for those who came to spend more than a few days.

John devoted most of his time to the building projects around the resort. He was particularly proud of the post office annex. He obtained the customer window and the mail boxes from the old post office in Havilah, the first county seat of Kern County. The same window and boxes are still being used in 1979.

When the post office was given official status in 1932, John became the postmaster and served for about ten years.

Marion managed and promoted the popular hot springs resort, as well as operating the store and overseeing the garage business. The feminine touch in the hotel and cafe was provided by Gwenevere Hooper, who also managed to support the South Fork Woman's Club projects and be an active member of the Kernville Methodist Church.

In 1930, Marion purchased a mining claim several miles up on Erskine Creek, near the Liebel Ranch. He made plans to mine the claim, in addition to running the resort. The Hooper energy was always in high gear — like father like son!

John and Marion rebuilt the hydroelectric plant in 1931 on the same site where Sherman had his plant in 1889. They salvaged an old water turbine that originally operated the stamp mill at the Mammoth Mine to power their plant. The installation supplied all the electricity used at the resort and continued to function, despite numerous floods, fires, and breakdowns until 1950. After the flood that year, the plant was closed down, and power was supplied to the resort by the Southern California Edison Company.

He converted the mill for custom work, and equipped it with a cyanide plant. The process allowed almost 100 percent recovery of gold and silver from ores by dissolving the gold and silver in weak solutions of sodium cyanide. The solution was then run through boxes of fine zinc shavings, the gold adhered to the zinc and was then separated from the zinc by heating.

John and Gwenevere on their 50th wedding anniversary. Son Marion and Grandson Richard in back.

The mill served the independent miners in the area, who brought quartz ore to be milled, or placer gold to be weighed. John assayed what they brought and bought their gold for whatever the going price of gold was at the San Francisco mint. He shipped the bars of gold amalgam to the mint and received payment from them. Those were Depression years. When cash was scarce, the miners redeemed their gold for groceries and supplies from Hooper's store.

PeeWee Oldham, 71, who claims to be the only placer miner working on the Kern River in 1978, first came to the Greenhorn Cave Mines in 1932. Pee Wee (Carl) looks like his nickname, but not like his years. He talks about the '30's with nostalgia, and recalls his dealings with

71

Honest John Hooper with affection. "John always treated me fair. Them was hard times, what with the Depression and Prohibition, too. A feller didn't need much, maybe $2.50 a month. Coffee only cost a quarter for two pounds. John always bought my gold for what the mint give him, and credit in the store if I come up short. He was a good man, we got along just fine."

Depression or not, things brightened up considerably in 1935, when Marion brought his new bride, Sally, to Hobo Hot Springs. Sally had been working as a legal secretary in Los Angeles before their marriage, and she was also a talented musician. Before long, she was playing piano with local bands, and music became a popular weekend attraction at Hobo Hot Springs. Sally and Marion actively promoted the resort, advertising the miraculous powers of the hot mineral springs baths. The clientele grew steadily, and the resort became well known throughout the county and the state.

While Marion and Sally attended to the details of running Hobo Hot Springs, John continued to devote all his time to custom mill work, until he broke his leg in 1937. The accident happened while he was working on the road to a new copper prospect. He was 67 years old — and still active and fiesty. By the time he was fully recovered, mining was at an all time low, so he sold the mill to the Moreland Mining Company, who dismantled it and moved it to their claim on the Piutes. The mill is still standing on the same mining site in 1979, the property of William Moreland of Kernville.

In 1939, Sally and Marion hired Thomas and Hilja Kopeka, professional therapists from Finland. They combined their expert knowledge of deep massage with the soothing effects of the hot mineral spring waters, and it didn't take long for the word to spread about the "miraculous" relief from aches and pains that all their patrons were receiving.

During those years, more than 2,000 people came to Hobo Hot Springs each year; many of them traveled from out of state to seek out the Kopekas. Hilja endeared herself to everyone, but her husband kept the guests and the Hobo Hot Springs community in awe. Perhaps it was Finnish tradition, but nobody remembers ever calling Kopeka by his first name. It was always deemed proper to call him "Mr."

Mr. Kopeka died in 1945, but Hilja remained at the resort until 1969, serving her loyal customers.

John and Gwenevere took a long vacation in 1940, visiting relatives in Virginia, seeing Washington, D.C., and the World's Fair in both San Francisco and New York. In 1942, he sold his interest in the resort to Marion and Sally, and "retired." He and Gwenevere moved to Kernville and John started another project, his final one. The last two years of his life were spent building a new home for Gwen. Marion remembers that many of John's friends warned him that he was too old — that he would never be able to finish the job. But he did. They had just moved in at the time of his death in 1944 at the age of 74.

Fred and Ruby Dodds came to Hobo Hot Springs as newlyweds in 1946. They fell in love with the little resort community and pitched in to help Sally and Marion make it even more successful. Fred managed the store and took over most of the trailer park maintenance duties. Ruby worked in the hotel and managed the restaurant. Small as the town was, there was plenty of work, and things were never dull. Once, the cook in the cafe attempted suicide. A Chinaman living in one of the cabins killed himself — not on the same day, of course. All in all, the hectic times were far outnumbered by the good ones. Fred and Ruby added another element of humor and friendliness, and business was good.

In 1947, Sally suggested that it was time to give the resort a new name. She chose Miracle Hot Springs, since it was the "miracle" powers of the hot springs mineral waters that continued to bring visitors back again and again. A petition was circulated among the residents, and the new name was accepted.

Miracle Hot Springs was initiated with a town celebration, highlighted by the mock hanging of the "Hobo." In November of 1947, the post office was officially changed to Miracle Hot Springs, and the Hobo stamp became a collectors' item. However, the riverside camp below the resort is still called Hobo Campgrounds, now maintained by the Forest Service.

In 1949, Fred and Ruby leased the resort from the Hoopers, and assumed the duties of new owners.

Sally and Marion moved into Kernville. Marion opened a rock and cement plant on the river and Sally worked in the post office. The 1950 flood washed out the plant, but Marion rebuilt it and ran it until 1952. He and Sally moved to Bakersfield, where she returned to secretarial work with the General Mortgage Company and also worked briefly in the advertising department of the *Bakersfield Californian*. In 1965, they moved to San Luis Obispo. Marion and his son, Richard, built a lovely home, and Sally worked for Great Western Savings until she retired in 1974.

In 1975, on their 40th wedding anniversary, the Hoopers were married again in a very special ceremony. Their sons, Richard and Daniel, both ministers, performed the wedding. The marriage certificate bore six Hooper signatures.

Daniel Hooper is a Lutheran minister in Phoenix, Arizona, and Richard Hooper carries on a specialized ministry in Pacific Grove, California.

Marion will soon be eighty years old, but he gardens and stays fit by dancing! Sally has returned to her first love — music — and plays regularly with a small combo. Marion attends every affair the combo plays for, and "dances up a storm," according to Sally. John Hooper's legacy of vitality is obviously alive and well.

When Fred and Ruby Dodds took over the operation of Miracle Hot Springs in 1949, they added two more hotel rooms on the third floor, and enlarged the kitchen facilities on the ground floor, then refaced the front of the building. The 1950 flood wiped out most of the trailer park and the cabins, and destroyed the power plant. SCE provided electricity to the resort, and Fred and Ruby began the job of rebuilding the trailer park, in addition to beginning a family and carrying on the business of the resort.

They had three children, Mike, Colleen, and Randy, who shared their parents' love for the little community, and put down their own youthful roots in the historic setting.

1954 was a big boom time for Miracle Hot Springs. In January of that year, Harry B. Mann discovered uranium deposits about one mile below the resort. It was like gold rush days again, only this time the fortune hunters carried Geiger counters.

All claims had to be registered with county offices by June 8, 1954. Ruby and Fred recall that for 24 hours before the deadline, Sheriff Gene Young and a 67 man posse stayed on patrol to keep claim jumpers away.

Fred and Ruby Dodds, 1968.

Three major deposits were worked through 1958. The Kergon, owned by Great Lakes Oil and Chemical Company of Bakersfield, with Charlie Hale as superintendent; The Miracle, owned by five Kern County men; and the Little Sparkler. The total yield from all three mines was eleven railroad cars of ore which averaged 0.3 U_3O_8 per ton. The Kergon still showed minor activity in 1978.

Miracle Hot Springs Resort buzzed with activity during the big uranium rush. Fred and Ruby took advantage of the good times and, in 1957, they purchased the Hoopers' interest in the resort and became full owners. In 1959, they built a small post office and a tackle shop across the road from the hotel. All the equipment from the Havilah post office was carefully installed in the new little building, and Ruby became the official postmistress.

No matter how busy the resort was, Fred and Ruby gave generously of their time and energy to many civic organizations in the Kern River Valley, including the VFW Post 7665, the Lake Isabella Chamber of Commerce, and the Kern River Valley Chamber of Commerce. Fred served on the board of directors of the Kern River Valley Hospital when it was still in the blueprint stage, and was re-elected to the board in 1978.

In 1968, the Dodds' made a major investment of $110,000 to build a modern Recreational Vehicle Park on the land originally used for small travel trailers. To counter the expected loss of visitor trade due to the construction of fourteen miles of four-lane freeway on the other side of the river, the couple planned to hold an annual Hobo Daze event each May. Hobo costumes, hobo stew in steaming cauldrons, games and dancing for the whole family, and a historical tour of the hotel grounds led by Marion Hooper, were planned events. The first Hobo Daze celebration was held in 1973, the second in 1974.

Tragedy nearly ended the Miracle Hot Springs dream in 1975 when the entire hotel building was destroyed by fire. Fred and Ruby were visiting in the midwest when the fire leveled the buildings.

In late 1977, the RV park boasted 49 spaces, all improved. The freeway had not stopped the fishermen from coming to their favorite haunt along the Kern River. Fred logged about 400 people in and out of the park during the summer, and about 50 during the winter months. Fred has plans to enlarge the park even further.

The little community looks barren without the familiar old rock-front hotel, but the people survived the shock and the loss by fire and rallied around to help in whatever way the could.

Ruby posts mail for 48 box holders daily in the little post office, and Fred opens the new store, now located in the tackle shop, each day for business. There's a pool table and a bright fire to welcome the "regulars" on chilly days. The Hot Springs family is still very much together.

Future plans for the resort are still pending, but there is plenty of good old-fashioned Hooper hope and Dodds determination in the air.

Even if the resort is never rebuilt, the same winding stretch of river will continue to draw campers and fishermen to its shores as it has for more than 75 years — and the Hot Springs community will make them welcome.

VI
Delonegha Hot Springs

THE SITE of the once busy and successful Delonegha Hot Springs Resort is located twelve miles southwest of Lake Isabella along the Kern Canyon Freeway, about one-half mile east of the last bridge that crosses the Kern River.

Early in the 1900's, the mineral spring health resort was a popular gathering place, but with the completion of a new road on the opposite side of the river between Bodfish and Democrat in 1905, Delonegha Hot Springs was bypassed, and business began to decline. By 1912 the resort was nearly deserted. As the years went by, the buildings were demolished, trees and bushes covered trails and clearings, and the only remnants of the resort that remained were two concrete bath tubs sunken into the hill just above the river. In June, 1977, the tubs were destroyed by the Forest Service for reasons of safety.

The name, Delonegha, first became familiar in the Kern River area in 1866 when Lovely Rogers, a native Georgian, and his partner, Hamp Williams, discovered gold there. Rogers called the new mining district, Dahlonegah, after the Georgia gold rush town of the 1830's by the same name. Dahlonegah was taken from the Cherokee Indian word, taulonica, which meant yellow metal.

In 1886, William Crawford homesteaded one-half section north of the Kern River around the hot springs, and named the picturesque riverside spot, Delonegha.

Crawford built a small house on the site in 1891 and brought his wife, Molly, and their three children, Mae, ten, and two younger boys, George and Willie, there to live. Once the family was settled, Crawford returned to his job in Bakersfield where he drove a hack and horse car for 75 cents a day.

Since there was no road through the Kern Canyon, the Crawford homestead was quite isolated. The nearest neighbor lived four miles up the side of Greenhorn Mountain, on a road that was little more than a wagon trail.

Some of the more colorful tales of the Crawford family during their residence at Delonegha were recounted by Mae Crawford Arnold in discussions with Charles Henning, a newsman, in 1965.

"Life wasn't peaches and cream at Delonegha," Mae recalled. "The best thing about it was the hot springs baths and lots of hot water to wash clothes in. Hot water poured out of the middle of big rocks and splashed into the river. I guess it still does. Papa built the bath house and the tubs on the edge of the river and piped water to it from a big spring up the mountain. The baths were fine, but most everything else was tough. Tough and steep. We had a tight cabin though and George and Willie caught fish in the river and we had a garden."

They also had four horses, fourteen goats, and 100 burros. Mae said, "I rode them jack-asses all over the mountains; we had a time with 'em though. The lions would kill them burros left and right. It got so at night when Papa wasn't home, which was most of the time, that Mama or one of us kids was out the door like a rocket when a dog let out his first bark, and them lions would hightail it!"

Times were made more difficult because Papa Crawford was often away for as much as six months at a time. Mae remembered that on those infrequent visits to his Delonegha home, her father had to come down over the Greenhorn Mountains on a "turrible road." The road was so steep that he had to chain the back of the wagon to a big tree to brake it against running over the team on the way down.

"Besides the lions that was always hangin' around hopin' to grab off a burro or a colt, every other creature born in the country came around to see what they could swipe, eat, scare, or disturb. Foxes and bobcats tried to get the chickens, coyotes stole what they could and kept us awake howlin', scorpions and rattlesnakes were always trying to share our beds, and the bears clawed into everything they wasn't meant to get at. Black bears, I mean. We knew that grizzlies didn't need no invitation for a fight — they'd come right out to meet you, but them little black bears, which was all over the mountains, was timid things and you could kill 'em with a stick."

The only other visitors the Crawford family had were an occasional homesteader or a miner who would build a raft on the opposite side of the river, shove it off about a hundred yards upstream, then pole across the swift river to the Crawfords' homestead. Since rafting, as well as swimming, was dangerous along this section of the river the visitors were few and far between.

The wild river didn't discourage everybody though. Mae Arnold recalled, "One man used to come over pretty often, Mr. Golf. He'd swim his horse across, sitting straight in the saddle all the way, and he never did have no trouble at all."

Sometimes the persistent Mr. Golf, who lived up on Breckenridge Mountain, made the crossing just in time to help Mae's mother butcher a goat.

Mae said, "Mama would always try to get Mr. Golf to take some of the goat meat to pay for his help, but he'd say, 'No, Molly, I don't want nothing but the head and the feet.' That's all he would take — every time. We never did know what he did with them heads and feet."

Mae said that when her father came home after being gone for a long time it was almost like Christmas. Not that there were many gifts, although he always brought something "unnecessary" for all the kids and for her mother, too. But it just seemed as exciting as Christmas because her father was there and the family was all together again.

One time, Mr. Crawford brought home a man known only as only as Costa Rica Joe. Mae remembered, "Joe was dying of TB at the County Hospital and somebody knew him that was a friend of Papa's, and when Papa heard about Joe he said he bet the good air and the hot springs

Mae Arnold, taken at Twin Oaks.

water baths at Delonegha, along with the goats' milk and goat meat and Mama's garden vegetables would cure him. So he brought Joe up there and it wasn't long before Costa Rica Joe was gettin' in the fire wood and doin' a lot of other chores around there. He lived for a long time. I don't even remember of him dyin' at all, but I suppose he did."

Homesteaders and miners frequently stopped by. When they did, they usually took baths in the bath house built by Crawford. After soaking in the concrete tub filled with hot spring water they would lie, blanket wrapped, on a sweatboard for an hour or so. Some of them would buy goats' milk or goats' meat, but they always left refreshed.

The sheepherders came to the Crawford homestead to buy the tough little burros that Mae herded. Mae said, "They're come clear over from Granite Station and even from down in the flat country to get our burros. Just about everything the sheepherders moved, except the sheep, was moved on burros' backs in them days. They'd pay as much as $50 for one of our jackasses."

Most of the homesteaders and miners carried guns of some sort; most of them were rifles with long octagon barrels. Mae continued, "We'd hear a little sometimes about somebody gettin' killed over claim-jumpin' or just arguin', but I don't think the law heard about it much of the time."

A murder took place nearby, involving two miners who were working a claim near Delonegha. Mae told the story, "One of them was Mr. Stokes and I don't remember the other one's name." She explained that after her father had visited with the family, he always took the two miners' gold back with him to the bank in Bakersfield. "They always brought it over in wax sealed fruit jars, and that made Papa nervous," Mae said. "He was always afraid the jars would get busted and he didn't want to be accused of helping himself to some. They knew exactly how much gold was there. They didn't trust each other too much, Papa said, and right up to the time the gold was sent off with Papa, each one was always weighing the jars and looking through the glass to make sure the other one hadn't added nothin' heavy to make up the weight of some swiped gold."

One day, Mae and her brother, George, were helping their father repair a corral, when Mr. Stokes came up to them and said, "I'm sure sorry I got to tell you this, Mr. Crawford, but I killed my pardner. I wish you'd come down there."

Mae went on with the tale, "John Monk, a cattleman from up on Greenhorn, and Sid Beavers, who had a homestead a couple of miles upstream, were taking baths and they went with Papa, Costa Rica Joe, and Mr. Stokes. They sewed Mr. Stokes' partner up in some sacks and buried him around there someplace. After the service — I guess you could call it that, I'm sure Papa must have said a few words over the poor man — Mr. Stokes left. He was probably afraid that word would get out to Granite Station and Bakersfield from Papa or one of the other men, so he didn't go out over the mountain.

"He'd made a raft, probably right after killing his partner and before tellin' Papa about it, and he got on his raft and went down the river. I can still see him as plain as anything. The last we saw of him, he was in a narrow place, pushing against the rocks on one side of the river with a long pole, and then real fast changing around and pushing against the rocks on the other side. We never did hear nothin' about Mr. Stokes again. We didn't know if he made it out of the canyon or not."

Although most of the travelers who stopped at Delonegha were welcomed, there was one frequent visitor with which Mae and her family could not cope. The Kern River.

Mae remembered, "In the four or five years we was at Delonegha, the river rared up the slope of the mountain at least three times and every time it come up, it took everything away. Everything except the house which was way up the mountainside on a scooped out spot. We had warning enough from the risin' of the river to get the burros and goats and chickens up the mountain, but we couldn't do nothin' about the bath house and the corral and the sheds. Everything would get washed away and then Papa would have to borrow the money to fix things up again.

"The last time we got flooded out, Papa mortgaged the Springs to H. H. Fish, the man he was driving a hack for in Bakersfield, so he'd have the money to repair things with."

Mae, who was 84 years old when she told the story, shook her head sadly, "Them was bad times. Things was tough with us, and when the mortgage came due, Papa couldn't pay and Mr. Fish said, 'Get goin!' He moved us like we was a bunch of rats. Mama cried, but Mr. Fish only said, 'Get movin.'

"Papa took us, jackasses and all, up to an old mining claim on French Gulch, near where Wofford Heights is now. It was even more uncivilized than Delonegha was, which is sayin' a lot. Not because there was less people around there, because they was more. There was a few characters minin' and bummin' in them mountains that would skull you for half a dollar.

"One time I was ridin' my special jackass down French Gulch on the road to Kernville and I saw spots of blood on the trail. I got off my donkey and tracked the blood spots, and pretty soon I found an Indian all drawed up behind a manzanita bush with his head darn near beat off. After a lot of strugglin' I finally got him to his feet and across my jackass and I took him down to the stream and cleaned his head off with a barley sack. He told me he'd got drunk in town on some two-bit wine and bragged to a couple of men about havin' four dollars, which he didn't, and somebody dry-gulched him on the way home."

About 1898, H. H. Fish leased Delonegha Hot Springs to Simeon Hill and his son, Dell. They built a hotel, boarding house, several dwellings, and a bath. Dell bought the land in 1903 and advertised the resort extensively as a health spa and headquarters for miners. It flourished for several years, particularly during the peak seasons of 1905 and 1906.

It was a perilous ride down the steep mountainside to the Springs. During the busy years, the Hills provided a stage for their guests, miners, mail, and supplies. Not without incident, however. It was a two day trip by stage over Greenhorn Mountain from Bakersfield, by way of Granite Station, and the rugged country was unpredictable. In April of 1908, there was a newspaper story that reported the Delonegha stage and four horses rolled 200 feet down a cliff. The passengers were able to jump free and escape "with varying degress of injury." Needless to say, the healing waters of Delonegha Hot Springs soothed most of the "varying degrees of injury."

As soon as winter and spring snows were gone, the Delonegha stage made regular trips over the nearly impassable roads, bringing visitors to the enchanting resort community situated at the opening of a canyon on the banks of the Kern River. Hotel guests paid by the week, ate at the boardinghouse and bathed in the effervescent waters of the mineral springs.

In spring, the hillsides around the resort blazed with orange poppies, blue lupine and stately waxen yuccas. The thick trees and mountain shrubs shaded the resort from the summer sun and in the damp, shadowed places near the springs grew a multitude of violets.

The mountain retreat is still a fond memory for Ida B. Pascoe, valley matriarch who celebrated her 99th year in 1977. As a small girl, she remembers the day-long horseback ride with her parents, Rev. and Mrs. O. D. Dooley, from their home in Woody down the mountainside to bathe in the hot mineral baths at the Springs.

Edgar Barbeau was the last person to manage Delonegha Hot Springs Resort as a business, but by the time he took over the heydays were ended. Mining was on a steady decline, and the new road across the river was much more tempting to travelers. By 1910, the resort hotel was closed, and all but a few residents had moved away.

In 1912, Jim Polkinghorne brought his bride, the former Leo Herzinger, who had been a schoolteacher at Bodfish, to the nearly deserted Delonegha settlement to live in one of the guest cabins while he completed a home on their 160 acre homestead across the canyon.

Jim widened an existing footbridge so that he could take a horse across the river to the building site. The new house was built on Mill Creek, in a grove of trees east of the road, and for many years it was a familiar landmark to travelers along the Old Kern Canyon Road.

Alfred James Polkinghorne was born at his mother's home, the McGuire Ranch in Walker's Basin. His mother was a native of the Kern River country, but his father came from Cornwall, England. Jim had one brother and four sisters, and they attended schools in Walker's Basin and Havilah. In 1893, Jim's father was killed by a runaway horse, and a short time later his mother remarried. It was not long afterwards that Jim struck out on his own and began his lifelong career as a cowboy.

Jim ran cattle in the Kern Canyon using his place at Mill Creek as headquaters and a second ranch in Havilah to hold cattle when they weren't on the range.

The ranges his cattle roamed were the steep, rocky hillsides along the Kern River. It took a special breed of cowboy to handle cattle in such rough country. There were only a few, and Jim Polkinghorne was one of the best.

He was nicknamed "Polky" by his friends, but the name was the only thing that was slow about him. Like any good cowboy, he could work slow and easy when the occasion called for it, but Polky was best known as one of the old time "brush poppers."

While gathering wild cattle on hillsides that looked too steep for a horse to stand up on, much less run, Jim would ride full blast off the top of a hill through a brush field that looked impregnable. The other cowboys always said that when Polky saw the color of a cow's hide, she was as good as caught! He always wore a heavy denim jacket and leather chaps and his saddle and the rest of his rig always looked like they had been through a war.

Jim seemed to have no fear, even when tackling the river at flood stage. He had never learned to swim a stroke, but if the river was running high and fast he would tie his lasso rope around his waist, leaving about eight feet from the other end of the saddle horn, sure that if he was swept out

Jim Polkinghorne

Remick Albitre saddles Red for another ride down into the Kern River Canyon, where he has been riding for 70 years.

of his saddle his horse would pull him on through to shore.

In 1941, Jim sold the Havilah ranch to E. L. O'Reilly and sometime later, O'Reilly also purchased the Mill Creek land. Mrs. Polkinghorne passed away in 1948, and Jim died in 1958, but whenever the old timers talk about the days of the wild brush cowboys, Jim Polkinghorne's name rates high on the list of the greats.

Cattle still grazed the rugged, brushy hillsides of Greenhorn Mountain in 1979. Remick Albitre, 77, one of the last of the wild brush cowboys, ranged his cattle on the north slopes between

Delonegha Hot Springs and Democrat Hot Springs. He passed away in 1978.

Remick first rode the Greenhorn range in 1909 when he took part in his first rodeo at the age of nine. In those days, cattlemen worked the range from a central location since there were no fences. Each day they worked a different section of the range together; each owner's calves were branded and his beef stock cut out.

Today, there are many fences dividing the mountain ranges, and lands are alloted to the cattlemen by the Forest Service. Cowboys, like Remick Albitre, work alone. They no longer share range time with their neighbors, nor do they share the easy companionship around an evening campfire after a long, hard day's work. Strong, hot coffee and tall tales were part of the joy of cowboying.

Remick describes his present allotment as a "big field." On the western edge, fences run northwest from Democrat Hot Springs up in the mountain towards Rattlesnake Grade. Fences on the eastern end of the allotment run northwest from Delonegha Hot Springs to the upper end of his range, which adjoins privately owned and fenced property. The southern border of Remick's allotment is the Kern River.

From his summer headquarters on Rancheria Road, high on Greenhorn Mountain, Remick still rides his allotment on the Forest Service reserve, where he has a permit to graze 100 head of cattle. Accompanied by his faithful cow dogs, always the mark of a good brush cowman, he checks stock on the familiar range and continues the legend of all those wild brush cowboys who challenged the rugged hills.

Remick Albitre, at 77, looks as tough and weathered as the land he loves. He is still a popular participant in local calf brandings, and he handles a rope with such ease and grace that it seems to come alive in his hands. His ancient saddle bears the scars of the thousands of brush patches that he has charged through in search of a wild cow. He has the roughened hands of a working cowboy and eyes that smile with the memories of good friends and stories about the untamed, wondrous early days of the Kern River country.

Prodding his memory a bit, Remick remembered visiting the Delonegha Hot Springs Resort in 1909 with his father, Bat Albitre, one of the pioneer cowmen on the Greenhorn range. He recalled the steep ride down the mountain from the cow camp to the Springs, the handsome hotel with wide, shaded verandas, and the bustle of guests. Even though business had begun to slack off by then, Remick described the resort as a most impressive sight to a wide-eyed nine-year-old.

Progress gradually by-passed the once thriving Delonegha Resort. Two new hotels, one at Hobo and one at Democrat, were built. They both featured hot springs baths and were built on the opposite side of the river. Since they were easily accessible to the public by means of the new canyon road, Delonegha was soon forgotten. The hotel was closed by 1912, and most of the small residences were vacated.

The last private owner of the land was Dr. B. N. Kershaw. If he had plans to rebuild the resort, they never materialized. The buildings were all torn down over a period of years, leaving no sign of the gracious retreat that once played host to miners, cowboys, teachers, preachers, and wide-eyed youngsters.

All that remains along that secluded curve of the river, are the great whispering trees and a tangle of undergrowth wound around the granite boulders. But the land where Delonegha once welcomed weary travelers must still cast a gentle spell. Rarely do I pass by on the busy freeway without noticing a car or two parked there above the river. The timeless beauty lives on.

VII

Democrat Hot Springs

NAMED IN HONOR of the local reigning political party, Democrat Hot Springs resort was built five miles below Delonegha Hot Springs on the south side of the Kern River.

In 1904 Delbert Hill, who, with his father Simeon S. Hill, owned and operated a hotel at Delonegha, saw the handwriting on the wall. A resort on the south side of the river would draw twice the business. The main reason for this was that it would be much more accessible. By this year a road had been pioneered by John Neil from Bodfish down the south side of the Kern Canyon as far as Democrat. It would be two years before this road would be finished. The Edison Company had also built a road down off Breckenridge to the headworks of the K.R. No. 1 Power Plant, and this was only a short distance from the Democrat Springs. Delbert Hill applied for and was granted a patent by the General Land Office in 1904 for the "OK" Placer Mining Claim, which took in fifteen acres around the springs, adjoined by Forest Reserve Lands.

By 1908 Hill had built a fifteen-room hotel at Democrat Hot Springs which with cottages placed nearby would accommodate 100 people. The lumber for all the construction was hauled by teams from the Dougherty sawmill on Breckenridge. This sawmill, started by Lloyd Lucas and operated by him until his death in 1873, also furnished the lumber for most of the construction in the town of Bakersfield.

There were five springs on the property. One of the springs flowed about twenty gallons per minute at 115 degrees Fahrenheit, and furnished an ample supply for bathing. Downstream, 400 yards from the main spring and near the hotel, a reservoir was formed around several more hot springs. This reservoir was covered, and used as an indoor plunge. The water contained iron, sodium, and other salts, but wasn't as heavy with minerals as the springs farther up river.

As with Delonegha, the main attraction besides the lovely setting along the river were the hot springs.

Dell and Augusta Hill continued to build the reputation of the resort. Casual visitors often became regular guests, and stayed for extended periods of time. Besides the hot baths the hotel was also famous for its wonderful meals.

To get to the hotel, guests traveled up the Breckenridge Road to Rock Springs Station and

The four horse stage leaves Democrat for Bakersfield.

A group of boys from the Democrat Hotel, 1909.

The boys from the Democrat Hotel show off some big ones.

after an overnight stop continued down the Cow Flat Road to Democrat. Although this road was better than the one to Delonegha, the trip was still no picnic, and the road was dubbed "The Nightmare Trail."

In 1913 Mr. and Mrs. A. M. Moberg took over the springs, and many of the local residents spoke highly of this family.

Rock Springs Station. This was the overnight stop on the trip from Bakersfield to the Democrat Hotel, and was located on the Old Breckenridge Road.

Jim Polkinghorne who, with his wife Leo, lived on Mill Creek just three miles up canyon, were two of the regular guests. Jim would invite friends of his from the Kern River Valley down to Democrat for a meal. One who remembers these

Empty whiskey kegs — Democrat Hotel.

POST CARD

DO YOU GET IT? NO! WELL LET ME "ELUCIDATE", THESE ARE A FEW OF OUR FELLOW VACATIONISTS CAUGHT IN THEIR FAVORITE PASTIME OF KILLING TIME, THE GAME THEY ARE "PLAYING AT" IS KNOWN AS "CROQUET" OR FIRST COUSIN TO THAT GRAND (?) OLD GAME "GOLLUF" OR "COW PASTURE POOL", THE PLACE? WHY NONE OTHER THAN DEMOCRAT SPRINGS "THE ATLANTIC CITY OF KERN COUNTY" LET ME STATE IN PASSING THAT "CROWKAY" IS VERY "PASSE"

AS EVER
"CHET"

JUN
15
1916
A.M

MRS. C.W. YOUNG
*27 FAIRMOUNT ST.
ARLINGTON
MASS.

POST CARD

HERE WE SEE IN THE DISTANCE THE PLUNGE AT DEMOCRAT SPRINGS OVERLOOKING THE PLACID WATERS OF THE SUNNY KERN, TO THE RIGHT IS THE POPULAR TANGO PALACE WHERE NIGHLY HAPPY CAREFREE COUPLES TRIP THE LIGHT FANTASTIC TO THE STRAINS OF THAT HAUNTING MUSIC OF AN ELECTRIC PIANO, SO ON WITH THE DANCE LET JOY BE "UNREFINED". IN MY NEXT ARTICAL I SHALL DWELL AT LENGTH ON OUR JUSTLY FAMOUS BOARDWALK DON'T MISS THIS ISSUE

BY-BY
"CHET"

MRS. C.W. YOUNG
*27 FAIRMOUNT ST.
ARLINGTON,
MASS.

Killed at Democrat Springs.

POST CARD

SEE THE "BULL MOOSER" HANGING OUT TO DRY, BUT THEN MOST OF THE "BULL MOOSERS" I KNOW ARE HANGING OUT AND DRY TOO JUST NOW, THIS IS A PRETTY NICE LOOKING BUCK AND THERE ARE SEVERAL IN THIS COUNTRY IF YOU KNOW WHERE TO LOOK GEO. ROSS CAN SHOW YOU TEN IN TEN MINUTES IF YOU WILL WALK A SHORT DISTANCE OFF "THE BEATEN TRAIL"

AS EVER
"CHET"

MRS. C.W. YOUNG
*27 FAIRMOUNT ST.
ARLINGTON, MASS.

POST CARD

I HATE TO BLAME THESE BOILS OF MINE ON SUCH AN INNOCENT LOOKING PLACE AS THIS BUT I DO, YES AND FURTHERMORE I BELIEVE THOSE TWO "JEW BOYS" McBRIDE AND McDADE KNOW MORE ABOUT THIS THAN THEY CARE TO TELL, McDADE SAID "THEY ARE WORTH FIVE BIG DOLLARS APIECE TO YOU", I SAID "ALL RIGHT ISADORE I WILL GIVE THEM TO YOU CHEAP, A DIME FOR ONE THREE FOR A QUARTER", BUT NO SALE

AS EVER,
"CHET"

JUN
8

MRS. C.W. YOUNG
*27 FAIRMOUNT ST.
ARLINGTON, MASS.

Simeon S. Hill and grandson, Dean, at Democrat Hot Springs, early 1900's.

trips fondly was Chet Young. Chet was the resident engineer on the Bodfish-Havilah Road, and the trips he made to this resort were recounted to his wife back east on the post cards. Opposite.

By 1913 the four-horse stage had been replaced by an auto stage. Guests were picked up at the Arlington Hotel on the corner of 19th and Chester in Bakersfield, and whisked over the 35 miles to the resort in a mere five hours. After Mr. Moberg passed away, his wife Anna continued to run the resort with the help of a son, Slim (Herman), and a daughter, Gertrude, who later married Morris Reeser.

There were many cattlemen who stopped by the Democrat resort for a meal and a drink when they were working cattle in the area. Some of the cowboys who looked forward to this pleasure in the old days besides Jim Polkinghorne were Remick Albitre, Cliff Record, Hugh Smith and Alex Silicz. Alex also took his young sons, Bud and John, with him on these trips. In 1978, the boys still remember the Moberg meals. Cliff

Record's son Glenn still runs cattle on the river at Democrat.

In 1959 H. W. Phillips bought Democrat Hot Springs, and after two years sold it to Don Adkinson.

Adkinson, after owning the property four years, traded his interest to Charles West for some ranch property. These owners listed above all made plans to again make Democrat Resort the attraction it was in years past, but their plans didn't pan out. Oscar Whittington was the last to try to revive the old spirit by bringing in live music for dancing on the weekends. He imported such well-known Western artists as Jelly Sanders.

Over the years there were hundreds of Bakersfield residents who enjoyed this picturesque spot along the Kern.

The owners in 1978 were three young men who enjoyed this spot in their high school days in the '60s, George Dewar, John Sanders, and Frank Jeppie, Jr. Because of previous vandalism the new owners hired an armed caretaker and furnished him a pack of junk-yard dogs to protect the property. There are gates as well to prevent anyone entering the property unless the owners are present.

It is still the same enchanting spot along the Kern River that it was almost eighty years ago. Spring still brings forth hillsides of poppies, lupines and the stately yuccas. The thick trees and mountain shrubs shade it from the summer sun.

It is reported the new owners plan to remodel the old hotel and rent it out to large companies for business seminars. So who knows — some day Democrat Hot Springs may again be in the news.

VIII

Kern River #1

UNTIL THE EARLY 1900's the stillness of the lower Kern Canyon was broken only by the hunting cry of the hawk or the dashing waters of the Kern River. Although there wasn't even an Indian trail up the Kern River Canyon in those early days there would be some activity in the spring and early summer of the year when the local cattlemen would ride down from Breckenridge or Greenhorn to gather cattle that were grazing there.

Then in 1902 the Edison Electric Company took over the preliminary work that had been started by the California Power Company in preparation for the building of a power plant two miles inside the mouth of the Kern Canyon.

By the spring of 1903 the roads needed for this project were completed. These included two miles of road up the Kern Canyon to the power house site, a road later called the Cow Flat Road, that tied into the Breckenridge Road and worked its way down to the head-works location. A third road started at the top of the hill above the Power House site and after following hog-backs and ridges in an easterly direction, tied into the Cow Flat Road.

This last road went into Camp Two, one of four camps used for the construction of the tunnel and headworks. Camp Three was almost inaccessible and was connected to the road above by an aerial cable 2,700 feet in length.

The twelve miles of trail that can be seen on the south walls of the lower Kern Canyon were also built by 1903. This trail started at the Power House No. 1 site and after going through Camp Two and Camp Three, continued to Camp Four, which was at the headworks location.

By February of this year a work force of 200 men were at work excavating twenty tunnels.

Also finished by this time was the installation of a construction power plant located one and one-half miles above the main power plant.

The only physical evidence that remained in 1979 was a 16' x 16' cement structure. The camp at the construction power plant was called French Town, and was almost inaccessible as there was no road in that section of the canyon. The heavy pieces of machinery, after being hauled out on the ridge above the power plant site, were brought down an almost impossible half mile by means of hoist, cable, and special built sleds. The remains of this steep trail can be seen on the hillside just east of what is left of the temporary power plant. The lower part of the trail was destroyed when the canyon road was built in 1925.

This power plant was capable of 600 horsepower and played an indispensable part in the construction of the permanent plant.

With the pressure of 10,000 volts, power was transmitted up and down the canyon to be used for many purposes. It was used to operate air-compressor plants so the men could use machine drills instead of drilling the rock on the tunnel with hand drills. Other uses were for pumping water, for powering the ventilating blowers at the mouth of the tunnels, and for lighting the tunnels and camps.

The construction plant was powered by two McCormick turbines, working under a net head of 45 feet, directly connected to two 150-kilowatt three-phase generators. Because of the natural water fall it was possible to install this plant using only 800 lineal feet of flume to bring the water to the turbines.

The roads leading from Bakersfield to the plant site and headworks location were kept busy with horse drawn stages, loaded to overflowing with men going to the job. Carriages

Site of the Kern River No. 1 Intake.

went back and forth carrying the khaki-clad superintendents, engineers, and foremen. Heavy wagons, loaded with provisions and building materials, crept toward the distant hill, pulled by strings of plodding horses.

At each camp, bunk houses, cook houses, and commissaries were set up. These were complete with electricity, supplied by the temporary power plant at French Town, and water that was in many cases piped for thousands of feet. A telephone line also tied the power plant site to the headworks location, and tied into each camp.

By the winding course the Kern River takes from the headworks to the power plant, it is twelve and a half miles, and the river takes a fall of almost a thousand feet. However, using a system of nineteen tunnels, the distance from the headworks to the forebay (just above the power plant) is only eight and two-thirds miles. As the tunnels fall at the rate of only 18 inches per thousand feet, or a total fall of 68 feet, this gives the water an accumulated descent of 878 feet from the forebay to the main power plant.

Temporary power plant used for the construction of the Kern River No. 1 Tunnels.

The four horse stage on its way to Kern River No. 1 during a period of high water.

The tunnels were filled to six feet six inches, giving them a carrying capacity of 410 second feet, or 20,500 miners inches.

Driving these tunnels through mountains of solid rock was a tremendous and costly undertaking, but this was offset by the fact that the conduit was permanent, and the cost of maintenance would be low. Though the first drilling in the tunnels had been by hand, once the construction power plant was set up at French Town pneumatic drills were used. Air compressor plants were set up at five locations, one using two 50-horsepower compressors and the other four 75-horsepower compressors.

It took over 90,000 feet of three, four, and six-inch pipe to supply tunnels with air for the pneumatic drills, and to operate the ventilators.

In order for the work to progress faster on the longest tunnels, adits would be cut into the tunnel line in several places. This would give a greater number of tunnel faces to be worked at one time. Tunnel Number Two, for instance, if worked from only two faces would be a continuous stretch of 9,217 feet, but by breaking it up in

four sections by adits, it gave eight faces to be worked instead of two.

Tunnel work, then as today, is probably one of the most dangerous professions, but the pay has always been a little above that of the outside jobs. There are always those who like this sort of work.

On each face two drilling crews would set up, each with a machine man and a "chuck tender" or all-around helper. The drills were each set up on a perpendicular steel column and the drill could be slowly cranked forward as it ate its way into the granite.

A starter drill 18 inches long was used to start the hole and sparks would fly as the steel started striking the rock at the rate of 300 strokes a minute. The drill steel was progressively replaced by a longer one until eight-foot drills were used. Before too long, 16 to 20 holes would be bored into the face, and ready for blasting powder. The type or character of the rock determined not only the number of holes, but also their angle and the amount of powder used. The

A crew ready for work in the tunnel.

Miners work the tunnels.

average amount of powder for each "shot" was 50 to 75 pounds.

After the drilling machines were moved back and the powder had been tamped into the drill holes the fuses were lighted. The men rushed to the open air to await the explosion.

There was no more peace and quiet on the lower Kern Canyon. With work progressing on twenty faces at once, and a total of three million pounds of powder being used for the combined tunnel work, the air was filled with one muffled boom after another.

As soon as the ventilator fans had cleared the air, the mucker went in to clear the tunnel of debris. Tracks were installed in the tunnel as work progressed, and cars loaded with broken granite were pushed out to the dump on the mountain side. Many of these dumps can be seen on the south walls of the Kern Canyon as you drive by on Highway 178.

There were also 1,705 feet of flume to build, to bridge the spots where ravines interrupted the tunnel line.

At the intake the dam, built on solid bedrock, rises 48 feet, and is 204 feet in length. The dam is 45 feet thick at the base, and seven feet at the top. Over 20,000 sacks of cement were used in the construction of the dam as well as hundreds of tons of crushed rock, sand, and steel.

A 600-foot drainage tunnel was burrowed beneath the north bank of the river. A 12 by 18 by 52 foot tower, to house the working apparatus that lifted the double gates for the drainage tunnel, was also built.

The concreting of the tunnels was also a major project. The 9 by 9 foot tunnels that were left by the miners reduced to a uniform width of 8 feet by concreting.

After many long months of preparation the concreting of the tunnel started in September of 1905. Wagon loads of cement and other necessary materials had to be hauled in by twelve-horse teams, or strings of pack mules.

During the completion of the concreting job, work was speeded up by using trucks to haul cement through the finished tunnels. A truck

Two loads of cement ready to start through the tunnel. Each truck carried a pay load of 2,000 pounds.

A truck is lifted to the top of the hill above Camp No. 1.

was hoisted over the aerial cable on top of the hill behind the power plant. With a truck and trailer hauling, two tons of cement at a time could be moved.

The biggest part of getting ready for the concreting was to bring in five rock crushers and get them into position. Weighing seven tons each they were hauled from Bakersfield by 16-horse teams. They were then loaded onto special built sleds. The sleds weighed 2,000 pounds each, built of pine; they were fitted with six-inch steel runners one-half inch thick. Then came the job of getting them down the steep mountain to the chosen site. There was a roughly built sled road, but it was only by the great skill of the head teamster named Farley that the load reached its destination. Pulled by eight horses the sled inched down the mountain. In one case it took a full week to get the crusher to its site, a half mile from the road, averaging about an inch a minute. The many sharp turns could only be negotiated by pulling on one corner of the sled until the load could be swung around. Snubbed to rocks and trees by means of ropes to prevent tipping or sliding, the crusher was finally in place. Next came the sand rolls, each weighing five tons,

90

Pause for milk break while packing wood to the hospital.

The concrete mixing plant.

along with cables and hoists to be put into operation. Water pipes had to be run to tanks. In the case of upper No. 14 tunnel, water was supplied from Lucas Creek, where the pipe was run 1,000 feet up the mountain through the tunnels to the plant — a total distance in excess of three miles. Electric motors, transformers, and wiring for telephone and electricity had to be installed. Each of the five crushers and mixers that were capable of averaging over 75 tons of mixed material an hour, were set up at the intersection of two tunnels so that work could be carried on simultaneously.

The concrete was laid three inches thick on the floor, and eight inches thick on the walls.

Specially constructed cars were used to haul the concrete through the tunnels, each with the capacity of eighteen cubic feet.

When two cars were loaded, they were pulled over the crooked little eighteen-inch track by a mule that picked his steps over and between the ties, his way lighted by the "bug" attached to the collar of his harness. Twenty miles a day was the average day's work for man and mule, and the only excitement was created when one of the mule's ears came into contact with one of the two live electric wires running along the roof of the tunnel.

During the year-and-a-half it took to concrete the tunnels, only six days were lost due to bad weather or breakdowns. Each night the carpenters would remove the forms from the concrete that had set, and erect them for the following day's work.

There were sixty men working in each concreting crew, and in a day they placed about 110 cars of concrete, as well as 50 cars of backfill in places it was needed.

The next step was the construction of the forebay. Much of the success of this part of the job, as well as that of the concreting job progress, was due to Mr. Fischer, junior partner of the contracting firm. He was in daily touch with his foremen, and at night the telephone by his bed placed him within reach of the farthest camp.

The saying "an army travels on its stomach," could well be applied to the K.R.-1 construction crew. Because of the far-flung locations of the four construction camps, the job of supplying good meals for more than 200 men was a marvel of coordinated efforts. Every sack of flour, every

Live Pork was packed in.

pound of meat, and every ounce of tea or coffee had to be hauled in wagons many miles across the plains from Bakersfield. Then, in many cases, these supplies had to be packed on the backs of mules or burros over narrow mountain trails leading to each camp site.

J. W. McIntosh, who recorded some of the history of the K. R.-1 construction, wrote:

"In Glass and Fischer's big kitchens, where the ranges burn all day long, there is every evidence of the culinary department of a modern hotel. There one catches the sweet rich odor of roasting meat and broiling steaks, the aromatic fumes of coffee. There is a clatter of dishes, a bubble of boiling soups and vegetables, and now and then the sharp clang of the triangle calling men to their meals, while gliding busily through it all are the Chinese cooks and helpers in their quaint dress, and those soft, sing-song voices low-pitched in nature's melody. Never idle, never slow, the Orientals plod methodically through the strenuous press of each day's duties and accomplish wonders in their line."

In addition to the three regular meals to be served every day, meals were prepared for the men whose shifts brought them in late in the afternoon and at night.

Lunches were prepared for those who could

not come back to the main camp. The procedure was described in the following paragraph:

"After breakfast, at the long kitchen table, the shining knives gleam, cutting whole roasts of cold beef, pink, sweet hams, and loaves of bread. At either end of the table is a pile of big yellow paper bags. Two slices of bread are deftly buttered, the ham or beef slipped between and in a twinkling a sandwich is ready for another paper bag. Two kinds of sandwiches, olives, or pickles, hard boiled eggs, squares of golden cake, a tempting quarter section of pie, all go to make each man's lunch, and then at last the sacks are filled. They are carefully piled into wooden boxes and trundled away on the mule cars to the tunnels."

The kitchen crew did all their own baking, and 700 to 800 loaves of bread came from their ovens weekly. Each morning for breakfast, were prepared over 2,000 biscuits, 4,500 hotcakes, and each week 3,000 pies were baked. The hungry crews consumed 350 dozen eggs a week, and 80 beef a month were slaughtered. Between two and three tons of apples were made into apple sauce each month to supplement the fresh fruit and vegetables that were in season. Although the camps were out in the wilds, every effort was made to give the men all the comforts of home.

J. W. McIntosh gave the following description:

"The long low dining rooms, with their white-washed walls, are clean, light, and well-ventilated. The rows of tables covered with shining white oil cloth are set with glistening rows of plates, cups, and saucers, flanked here and there with a mammoth coffee pot, well-filled sugar bowls and cream pitchers, a big jar of pickles and bottles of catsup, and well-stacked bread plates."

In the commissaries, which were also operated by the contractors, the men could purchase anything from a sack of tobacco to a suit of clothes, and summer and winter they ran mail and passenger service from Bakersfield.

On October 1, 1902, the hospital was established at Camp Two, under direction of Dr. Milbank Johnson, head of the Edison Company's medical department. It was comprised of the main building, containing ten beds, a small room, bathroom, nurse's apartment, and the drug room. The hospital was supervised by Dr. H. C. Stinchfield, who rode back and forth between camps, treating those who didn't require hospital care, and keeping a check on the sanitation of

The hospital.

the sleeping and eating facilities in each camp.

Of the seventeen deaths that occurred during the four years of construction, only two died in the hospital. Five of the seventeen deaths took place on December 7, 1906.

Just about three weeks from the time the new plant was to be placed in operation, there took place one of the most dramatic rescues that ever happened in the Nation. Lindsay B. Hicks, one of the miners working for the Edison Electric Company, was trapped in a cave-in along with five of his co-workers. The five included Gus Anderson (foreman), George Warner, John Wible, H. Farris, and C. D. Robles, who were killed instantly, only Hicks surviving. The accident happened while the workers were in the process of putting the heavy steel and concrete lining in the shaft which was to carry the water from the forebay down to the power plant 1,661 feet below. The shaft had been mined upward from the bottom with the walls supported by timbers cut and fitted end-to-end to form a succession of octagons placed against the earthen sides of the shaft, wedged tightly to hold them in

place without nailing or cross braces. Sections of steel tubing were installed in the same manner from the bottom up. First, the bottom sections were placed. Concrete was then tamped between the steel and the shaft. Work and progressed until there was only 120 feet of shaft to be fitted with the steel tubing and concrete. On the morning of Friday, December 7, the progress of the workmen below made it necessary to remove the next set of timbers further up the shaft. To accomplish this, a crew of five men led by the foreman, Gus Anderson, were sent down the shaft from the top. Anderson ordered one of the men to loosen the lowest set of timbers without first blocking the timbers immediately above. Though some of the workmen felt it was not safe, they followed orders, and removed the wedge that released the bottom timber. Since these sets of timbers form octagons which were held together only by being wedged tightly against the walls of the shaft, when the first set of timbers collapsed, a cave-in began that triggered the release of the second set of timbers. As this let down more earth it released the third octagon.

Concreters in the shaft.

When the second set of timbers fell, the six men turned to flee up the steep incline of the shaft. The collapsing timbers, one after another, like dominoes, knocking each other over in a row, was too fast for the men, and they were caught like rats in a trap.

Hicks was in the middle of the group of men. He was struck by a falling timber just as he reached a skip, a small car used to haul concrete. Hicks was knocked forward beside the car, with the timber pressing on his back. The whole mountain seemed to thunder down, closing him in.

In an exclusive dispatch to the *Los Angeles Times*, released December 8, 1906, the headlines read, "No Hope For Entombed Men," and the sub-heading stated: "Will Take Ten Days Digging To Reach Bodies," "Coroner Will Not Visit Scene For Two Weeks," "Accident Said To Be Due To Miners' Carelessness."

The men on the job gathered around the collapsed shaft in horror, waiting silently as the tremendous task of exhuming the bodies began. Seventy hours had passed when, as the muckers were digging away at the top of the shaft, Pearl Davis, a shift boss, heard a faint tapping that seemed to come from deep within the earth. The signal was answered, and again came the far away "Rat-tat, rat-tat-tat" from the imprisoned miner.

Who could it be? Who could have survived instant death, to remain buried alive in the bowels of the earth?

Like an electric shock, the news spread. To the far corners of the earth it was known that one man, maybe more, was living in an earthen tomb.

All work on the great Edison power system stopped in the Kern mountains. Every available man was rushed to the scene. High officials of the company camped on the ground. Expert engineers helped with hands, and advice. The chief engineer was called from Denver. The men worked in a frenzy. It was four days after the cave-in that communication was established between the buried miner and the men who were now keyed to the highest tension to effect his rescue. This is how it was accomplished: The engineers, with great skill, pushed a steel pipe through the intervening debris and rock.

Lindsay B. Hicks. That is the name which, like an echo from another world, came to the rescuers.

Lindsay B. Hicks, sole survivor, cheerfully called to God's bright world that he was "all right."

Through that pipe lay an open path to the tomb, and through it men called messages of cheer to the buried man. A phonograph was installed and the dancing notes of ragtime resounded against the buried tram car which had saved Hick's life, and which still might become his coffin.

Milk was poured down the tube to keep the imprisoned man alive.

General Superintendent W. S. Cone of the Edison Electric Company came from Los Angeles to oversee the rescue. The best miners, and the cleverest engineers, were summoned from each of the camps. The Edison company paid all the men engaged in the rescue work double pay, and spent more than $30,000 for Hick's rescue.

Plans for digging down from the top of the caved-in shaft were judged not only unsafe for

Hicks, but also for the rescue crew. A tunnel was started in the shoulder of the mountain, a little below and about ninety-six feet from where the buried miner lay. The mouth of the new tunnel was over 1,600 feet above the river bed. The angle of the slope was 45 degrees and the tunnel had to start on the face of a precipice so steep that scaffolding had to be built from which to start the work.

The new tunnel had to go through the earth and decomposed granite. It had to be timbered nearly all the way. When nothing else stopped the progress, the miners would run up against a boulder and, if it could not be cracked, they would have to mine around it. The miners worked in frequent shifts, and pick handles never cooled.

In the tenth day of the heart-breaking work, the rescuers came upon a great wall of granite. It could not be blasted away. It had to be carefully bored by hand. Despair almost overtook the forces.

The twelfth day, December 18, Hicks seemed to lose his nerve. He broke down and wept, his racking sobs echoed faintly through the long pipe. He complained of the cold, and seemed terror-stricken, as though for the first time he had lost all hope.

Some had maintained all along that he could not live and remain sane, and even physicians on the scene feared that the man might become a raving maniac before he could be rescued. He had been coiled under the protecting tram car for thirteen days, with the decaying bodies of his former comrades almost within reach. The rats had already started devouring the dead bodies, and at times swarmed over his own body.

The next day Hicks was talking cheerfully again, and it looked like rescue crews would reach him in a few hours. But again fate intervened, and the rescue was postponed. December 21, the 15th day, passed and rescuers were so close to Hicks that they could talk to him directly, but then a mass of debris threatened to fall and not only further bury Hicks, but his rescuers also.

Risking all, they continued. Finally at 11:25 A. M. on December 22, sixteen days after he was buried, Lindsay B. Hicks was released from his living tomb. As soon as the last cut was made, the way was open, and Hicks began to scrape away rocks and dirt and crawled towards the opening.

Lindsay Hicks on the right talks to Dr. Stinchfield after being released from his tomb.

With arms in front of his head, he entered the miniature tunnel, and began to work his way to the other side of the car. After a short stop to catch his breath the man of iron moved a little farther toward freedom, and Dr. Stinchfield and a miner by the name of Gent, grasped him by the arms and pulled Hicks out into the main tunnel.

Dr. Stinchfield asked Hicks if he thought he could ride the old horse to the company hospital, six miles through the tunnel. "Just get me out of here, doctor," replied Hicks, "and I'll ride a wild mule there."

Of Hicks, it was said that he spoke intelligently. He had not aged perceptibly. His hair had not turned grey. He had not the look of a frightened man and to the best eye, it seemed that Hicks had just come from a hard day's work in a coal mine. He was dirty, his clothes were threadbare and worn in places. But above all he was game. He appreciated his "regeneration" for

Armature housing for the generator at the Edison Company Powerhouse Number 1. The gross weight of this load was seventeen tons and as it approached the mouth of the Kern Canyon 52 horses were needed to move it over the sandy roadway.

he said, "Oh, this is fine, boys, to be among you after spending an enforced rest on duty in that abominable hold. You fellows made it pass joyfully for me and at times I really believe I enjoyed my imprisonment. The thought that so many people were interested in my unhappy fate and were striving vigorously to get me out was a constant source of satisfaction. You can't realize how I appreciate your efforts.

"The sound of those picks and the saws was good to me, and when that plug of tobacco and the hearty handshake came through under the car this morning, I was truly happy. It seemed like a thousand year's burial under that awful mess. It's all over now, and I can only thank you and return thanks to God for my deliverance."

Wide interest had been shown throughout the nation during his ordeal. From Louisville, Kentucky, a wholesale liquor house requested its local distributor to send a case of whiskey to Hicks and his rescuers. By express, from San Francisco, came a ten-pound box of Star tobacco, Hick's favorite brand. Many messages and packages arrived at the Edison Camp for Hicks, and there was a theatrical offer from W. H. Brown of San Francisco, waiting for Hicks when he stepped into the daylight.

When word was received in Bakersfield that Hicks was out of the ground, the fire-house bell started clanging, and within five minutes every whistle in Bakersfield, the city of Kern across the river, and the oilfields, had joined in announcing the release of the man who had lain in his tomb for nearly sixteen days. Shotguns and revolvers were fired, men rushed into the streets and cheered. For more than half an hour there were revolver shots and shouting, the tooting of whistles and the ringing of bells, all testifying to the general rejoicing that the rescue work had been successful.

Of course Hicks went on stage, and his first appearance was in the Armory in Bakersfield. An

Miner Lindsay B. Hicks.

Camping for the night with armature housing on the way to the Kern River No. 1 power plant.

ordinary sitting room would have held the crowd. He fell as flat in Los Angeles and everywhere. Hicks, buried alive, with heroic men risking their lives to save him, was an object of material interest, but after Hicks was rescued, he dropped back to his old place and importance.

He was just another mucker, no different from all the other men who might be carrying a hod, or sweeping streets. Hicks married a widow and passed permanently from his brief pedestal of public prominence to the common land of domestic obscurity.

The last time Hicks' name appeared in the news was a few years later, when he committed suicide.

After Hicks' rescue, the men went back to the construction of the pressure main. For its entire length of 1,661 feet, the pressure main was an underground shaft, and lay from 50 to 100 feet beneath the surface of the mountain.

This shaft was then lined with a tapered steel tube that graduated from 90 inches to 28 inches and averaged an inch in thickness.

The entire length of pipe weighed over a million pounds, and over fourteen tons of rivets were used to fasten it together. From Camp One the pipe was hoisted in ten foot sections over the 1,700-foot cable to the top of the hill. It was then moved to the mouth of the shaft, and after being set on rollers, it was slowly lowered into place.

From a glowing red forge that blew and spit close by, riveters were furnished rivets for their pneumatic hammers. It took six to twelve hours to rivet the 18-inch straps that coupled the two sections of pipe. The concreters then took over and filled in the 75 to 80 cars of concrete needed to completely encase the pipe.

The power plant, with its steel frame and concrete foundations and walls built on solid bedrock, was covered with a corrugated iron roof, and was the last part of the construction.

The water, which has a perpendicular head of 877.35 cubic second feet comes into the power plant through feed pipes running beneath the floor of the main dynamo room, directly to the main impulse wheels.

Here the power was generated in four units, each unit operated by two overhanging impulse water wheels, carrying 18 bronze buckets against which the water directed a pressure of 380 pounds to the square inch.

In May of 1907, the power house, the last of the work to be finished was completed, and the power was turned into the receiving station at Los Angeles over 117 miles of transmission line. This line operated at a pressure of 75,000 volts, the highest ever attempted over such a length of cable.

While water power had been used in California even before 1847, when John Sutter used it to power his sawmill, in later years of energy related problems, the Kern River Plant No. 1, and many others, stand as testaments to the resourcefulness of Henry Sinclair and those who at the turn of the century had a vision of this great energy source which had little if any impact on the ecology.

The lower Kern Canyon still holds the same magic it has for countless ages. First for the local Indian tribes who fished along its shaded banks, and later for the white miners who searched its shifting sands for gold.

The building of Isabella Dam has harnessed the destructive power of the lower Kern River during the flood stage, but the river still has many sections where the calm surface hides a dangerous undertow that each year claims the lives of a few of the unwary.

For those who exercise a minimum of caution, enchantment is still found along the Kern River today. Whether it be the springtime when the canyon walls are splashed with a rainbow of color from wildflowers, warm summer days when each bit of shade is welcome, or fall with its many shades of gold and orange. Each season holds its special charm in Kern River Country.

Bibliography

BOOKS AND PAMPHLETS

Bailey, Richard C. *Explorations in Kern*. Bakersfield, California. Kern County Historical Society, 1959

Bailey, Richard C. *Kern County Place Names*. Bakersfield, California. Kern County Historical Society, 1967.

Boyd, W. Harland. *A California Middle Border*. The Kern River Country. Havilah Press, 1972.

California State Mining Bureau, Sacramento, California. State Printing Office.

Hughes, N. Guy. *Lynn's Valley Tales and Others*.

Morgan, Wallace M. *History of Kern County, California*. Los Angeles, California, Historic Record Company, 1914.

Powers, Bob. *North Fork Country*. Los Angeles, California. Westernlore Press, 1974.

Powers, Bob. *South Fork Country*. Los Angeles, California, Westernlore Press, 1971.

Walker, Ardis M. *The Rough and the Righteous of the Kern River Diggins*. Balboa Island, California, Paisano Press Inc., 1971.

NEWSPAPERS

Bakersfield — *Kern County Weekly Courier, Kern County Weekly Gazette, Kern County Californian, Southern California, Southern Californian*, and *Kern County Weekly Courier, Bakersfield Californian*.

Havilah Miner, Weekly Courier.

Visalia Weekly Delta

MANUSCRIPTS AND PERIODICAL ARTICLES:

Rakin, Nana. *My Impressions of Early Days*.

Wortley, Ken. *Sierra Rainbow*, May and June, 1955. "Saga of a Sheepman." Kernville, California.

Index

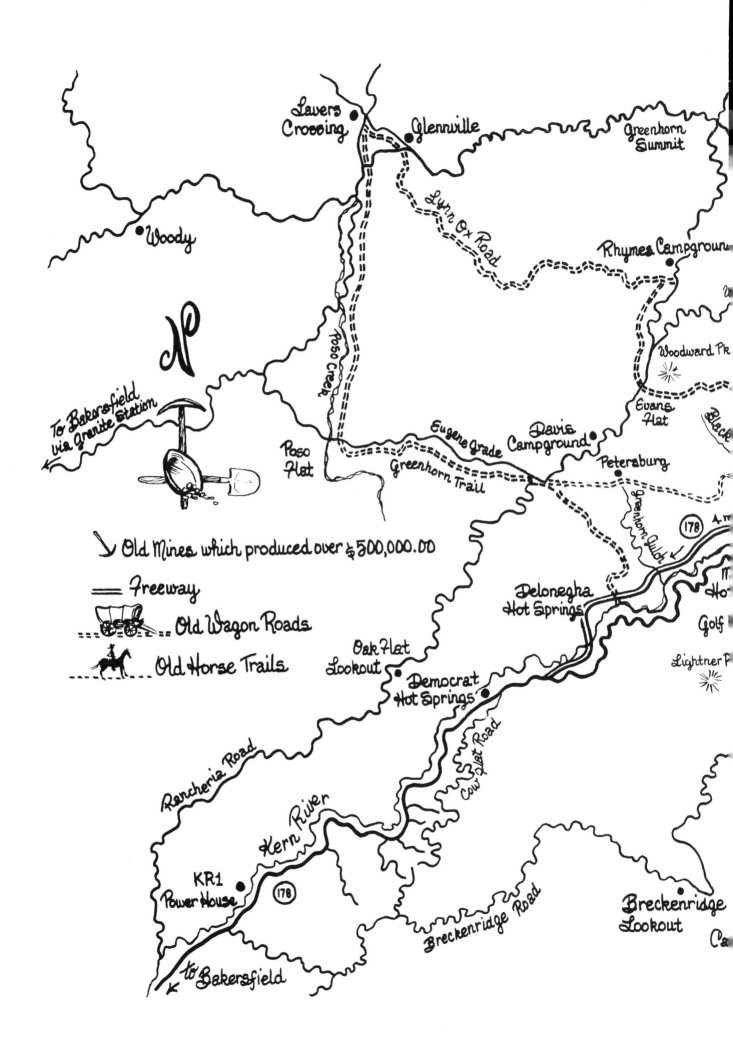